Successful Market Penetration

Successful Market Penetration

How to Shorten the Sales Cycle By Making the First Sale the First Time

Mack Hanan

American Management Association

This book is available at a special
discount when ordered in bulk quantities.
For information, contact Special Sales Department,
AMACOM, a division of American Management Association,
135 West 50th Street, New York, NY 10020.

Library of Congress Cataloging-in-Publication Data

Hanan, Mack.
    Successful market penetration.

    Includes index.
    1. Selling.   2. Selling—Key accounts.   I. Title.
HF5438.25.H353 1987   658.8′105   87–47704
ISBN 0-8144-5934-X

Printing number

10 9 8 7 6 5 4 3 2 1

To **John Malone**
>   And his "Marketers of The Midway"
> Who took for themselves
>   The challenge of working way out
> On the leading edge of
>   Penetration
> Long before it had penetrated
>   The consciousness of others
> To make it comfortable and urgent
>   To do so.

Preface

What is the ideal penetration strategy? It is to get into business with customers at the highest margins in the shortest time at the least cost—in other words, to condense the costly part of the sales cycle and expand the profitable part of the work cycle. How can we approach this ideal? There is only one way. We must change the way we approach the customer—to come at him side by side, as partners, instead of confronting him head to head as adversaries. This means first running to catch up, then adjusting our pace to his, and finally taking the lead. In this way, penetration is more likely to begin with the "ah-ha" of recognizing common objectives than the "uh-oh" of defending against being sold.

Penetration begins with being cooperative and contributory, not competitive. It means helping the customer sell his own products instead of closing him to buy from us; it means adding value to the customer's business instead of adding, then attempting to justify, a new cost.

Penetration does more than begin our business—it defines our business. It tells at once whether we are vendors of goods and services or partners in profit; cost-adders or profit-improvers; quota builders or customer builders.

Making the customer buy is one kind of penetration objective. Making the customer more profitable is the other.

Author's Note

Although market penetration is a genderless skill, so far in business more men than women have had the opportunity to show their prowess. This is acknowledged by the use of the pronoun *he* and its derivatives as a generic reference to penetration strategists throughout this book. Strategists who are women should have no reluctance about reading themselves into this simplified construction. By their unique creativity and dedication, it is only a matter of time before they equalize its underlying composition.

Contents

Successful Market Penetration

1

Developing the Strategy

Grasping the Essential Thrust of Life Cycling

Sales strategy is judged by a single criterion: *Are we making more money this year than a year ago?* To be able to answer yes, one of the most important things we can do is to condense our sales cycle—to shorten the mean time between penetrating our customer businesses and getting the order. This is the key to our rate of gaining market share. It is also the key to our cash flow and our ability to control the cost of sales.

The faster we can penetrate, the faster we can turn over the sales cycle. The faster we turn the sales cycle, the higher our chance for market leadership and the lower our ratio of investment to revenue. If, in the process, we find the way to command a premium margin for what we sell, turning over the sales cycle faster will enable us to multiply our profits exponentially.

What do we know beyond a doubt about penetrating our customers? We know two things. If we position ourselves as alternate vendors, differentiating our offerings principally on price, we know that we slow down the sales cycle. We require our customers to compare our product performance feature by feature and benefit by benefit so that we, and they, can justify our price. On the other hand, we know that if we position ourselves as consultants, differentiating ourselves by our ability to improve customer profits, we can accelerate our sales cycle. Our customers will be motivated to have their profits improved as quickly as possible by the pressure put on them from the time value of money.

Penetrating the way vendors sell threatens to contribute an added cost to customer businesses. As a result, it pays customers to take the time to try to reduce it. Every day of bargaining that goes by can mean an eventually lower price. Penetrating as a consultant puts a premium on time. The profits that a consultant can contribute can be put to work as soon as they are received. They are always worth more today than if they were received tomorrow. So it pays customers to acquire them at once. Every day's delay incurs an opportunity cost that subtracts from their value. Procrastination, the thief of time, then also becomes the thief of value.

The act of bearing new capital to our customers—not our products or services but their dollar values when they are applied to customer businesses—is the fastest way to be invited in. Unlike products, every customer is constantly in the market for incremental profits. No business can ever have enough.

If we penetrate as a consultant, we know *what* we must sell: new profits. We also can predetermine *how* we must sell—we must add the values of our incremental profits to a customer's business in the same places and in the same ways that the customer himself is trying to add value. If we do this, we cannot go wrong. If we address ourselves to the places in customer businesses where profits are most important, even imperative, we will always be talking to their priority objectives. If we address ourselves to these objectives in the same ways they do, we will always be compatible with customer strategies. We will make it comfortable as well as urgent to do business with us.

If we sell into our customers' topmost objectives with strategies that are familiar and acceptable to them, we can present ourselves as truly incremental to customer managers. In other words, we can gain acceptance as their natural partners in profitmaking. This is the only definition of partnership that has any meaning for a customer, because it expresses the only reason a customer will partner with us: We must add values to his business that he cannot otherwise obtain.

Penetration strategy therefore rests on the answer to one question: *Where in a customer's business can we add the most vital values?* The customer has already asked this question. Our answer must be: *At the points in his business life cycle that contain the greatest opportunities or the most necessary remedies.*

Customer Needs Throughout the Life Cycle

A life cycle is the curve a business makes as it moves through commercialization. Each life-cycle stage of a customer business predicts its needs. *Where* it is in its cycle predetermines *what* needs it offers for our penetration.

Each customer business need represents a value. Each value represents a worth in dollars. If a business is just starting up, its needs will be concerned with future values. These will include costs to be avoided and productivity and sales objectives to be ensured. If a business has already entered its market and is growing or has become mature, its needs will be concerned with both present and future values. These will include costs to be reduced, productivity to be improved, and sales to be gained or made more profitable.

All startups have similar needs, regardless of their differences in products or services or systems, regardless of their industry, regardless of the markets they sell to. The same is true for all new business entrants, all growth businesses, and all mature businesses.

In some industries, starting up takes longer than in others. From industry to industry, growth may be prolonged or foreshortened. Maturity may come sooner or later, may endure for a longer or shorter period of time. These differences are without distinction as far as penetration is concerned. Only the similarities at each life-cycle stage are relevant. If the needs they reflect can be benefitted—that is, if the problems they present can be solved and their opportunities capitalized—the customer who has the needs can be penetrated by a supplier who can benefit them.

Whenever we can avoid a cost or ensure productivity or sales for a customer startup, we can penetrate. Whenever we can reduce a cost or improve productivity or sales for a growing or mature customer, we can penetrate. As long as a customer's investment in the values we can add exceed his cost of capital, we can penetrate.

Startups are full of planned costs that can be avoided and planned sales that need to be ensured. Ongoing businesses are full of current costs that can be reduced or eliminated and planned sales that need to be increased. These costs and sales objectives are inherent in a business because they are part and parcel of its life-cycle phases. Tell me your life-cycle phase, we can say, and I will tell you where your unnecessary costs are and what opportunities you have for profit improvement. We will never lack penetration opportunity if we can do these four things:

1. Take a startup's proposed costs and reduce them by substituting lower costs.
2. Take a startup's proposed productivity and sales and increase them by substituting higher productivity and sales objectives.
3. Take the actual costs of an ongoing business and reduce them by substituting lower costs.
4. Take the actual productivity and sales of an ongoing business and increase them by substituting higher productivity and sales values.

Penetrating a customer business through the entryway of its present life-cycle phase is a tradeoff of value for value—our higher value for the customer's current or proposed value. Where costs are concerned, the customer's values will almost always be higher than the values we can trade in the operations where we are expert. With productivity and sales, the customer's values will almost always be lower. Our improved values certify our expertise as specialists in profit improvement. By expressing them in dollar terms, we can quantify our values as incremental earnings, true added values for our customer businesses.

In effect, we can say to our customers: Here are the values of your operations without us—negative values from unnecessary, avoidable costs and opportunity losses in productivity and sales. Now look at these same operations through our capabilities. Here are the added values we can bring to them— reduced negative values from costs and increased positive values from improved productivity and sales. The difference between the two sets of values represents the added value of doing business with us. If these values are worthwhile to you, we can begin to add them to your business at once.

The worthwhileness of our values is easy for customers to calculate. For a startup, it is the dollar value that accrues when it is able to enter its market sooner than planned. It is the dollar value that accrues to an entrant when it is able to reach its breakeven sooner than planned. It is the dollar value that accrues to a growth business when it is able to grow faster than planned. And, finally, it is the dollar value that accrues to a mature business when it is able to maintain its margins longer than planned.

In short, our worthwhileness is determined by our ability to contribute new values to the existing values of our customer's objectives. If we can form a strategic alliance with our customer businesses, we can penetrate them as partners: fellow value-bringers whose contribution is greater than the investment to acquire it.

Why, our competitor may ask customers we penetrate in this way, do they choose to do business with us? There are higher-performing products, or equals, at similar prices. There are cheaper products, some even higher in performance. Why us? With an eye to the values we add to their top and bottom lines—to their sales and their profits—our customers can give us the best reference in business: "We do business with them *because we have to.*"

Points of Departure for Penetration

Figure 1-1 shows the four stages in the classic business life cycle. The figure relates sales growth to time, starting out with negative growth, then moving to a positive sales and profit flow, and eventually showing how a negative rate of growth can overtake both sales and profits at maturity.

This basic visualization of the business cycle will be our touchstone to penetrating customers as their growth partner at any stage of their commercial life.

In scoping our opportunity to penetrate a customer business, we should form the habit of asking three questions about it, up front, before we do anything else.

The first question is, *What business is he in?* This gives us the chance to assess if the *customer's industry* is growing or mature.

The second question is, *What businesses are his major customers in?* This gives us the chance to assess if the *customer's main markets* are growing or mature.

The third question is, *What is the trend of his rate of growth over the past three years?* This gives us the chance to assess if the *customer's business* is growing or mature.

If a customer's industry is growing, his business is likely to be growing too; if his industry is mature, he is more likely to be mature.

If a customer's major customers are growing, his business is likely to be growing too; if they are mature, he may, nevertheless, be growing or he may be, like them, mature.

If a customer's rate of growth is growing, his business is growing; if it is stable or declining, he is likely to be mature.

A Business in Startup

These evaluations, general though they are, give us our point of departure for penetration. Let us take a new startup venture within a mature corporation. Without knowing anything more, just that it is a startup, we know what the manager's objective must be. He must move quickly through his

Figure 1-1. Life-cycle business opportunity curve.

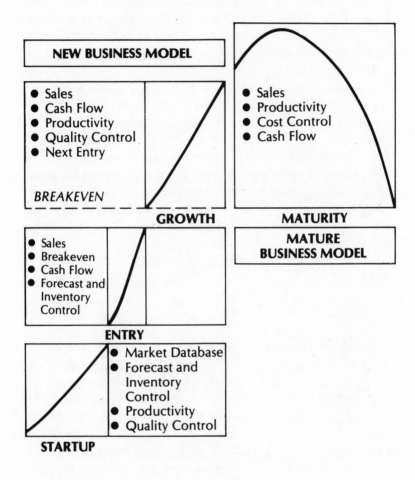

startup cycle, move "out of the garage" and into his market as soon as possible. He is on a borrowed budget and on borrowed time. His management will wait only so long for him to produce results. His competitors are not waiting at all. Meanwhile, for every day that passes, his market opportunity window may be closing.

What approach should we take? What is the first thing we should say? We must address the business life cycle. Since we know that market entry is a startup manager's fixation, our dialog should focus on it. Can we help the manager make entry on time? Even better, earlier? Less expensively? Can we help him stay there once he gets there by ensuring his product's reliability and avoiding recall? Can we help him make sure he is choosing the right "there"—that he has targeted the right market and positioned himself properly in its perceptions?

Our answers will be the basis for our penetration of startups.

A Business at Entry

Let us take a customer business that is just entering its market: a successful startup. Without knowing anything more, just that it is an entrant, we know what the manager's objective must be. He must consolidate his precarious initial toehold into a firm foothold by reaching breakeven and bringing in positive cash flow. Every unnecessary day below breakeven adds to costs, postpones profits, and increases vulnerability. His management's patience may run out or a competitor may become profitable first and plow back the profits into accelerated sales and advertising. The market's money may go elsewhere.

What approach should we take? What is the first thing we should say? We must address the business life cycle. Since we know that breakeven and the onset of positive cash flow are an entrant manager's fixations, our dialog should focus on them. Can we help the manager enter faster? Less expensively? Can we help him maintain his product within specifications and in stock? Can we help him bill and collect receivables faster to guarantee cash flow? Can we help him remain differentiated from the inevitable knockoff competitors who will be attracted by his success and unencumbered by his costs?

Our answers will be the basis for our penetration of entrants.

A Business in Growth

Let us take a customer business that is growing: a successful entrant. Without knowing anything more, just that it is growing, we know what the manager's objective must be. He must continue to grow at an ever-increasing rate. If his rate of growth slows, maturity may overtake the business and the opportunity to become a big winner will be foreclosed. If the market for the business is growing and the customer's industry is growing along with it, then each dollar of unmade sales growth represents opportunity loss that can never be made up.

What approach should we take? What is the first thing we should say? We must address the business life cycle. Since we know that the business growth rate is a growth manager's fixation, our dialog should focus on it. Can we help the manager ensure productivity, minimize downtime, and assure consistency by manufacturing a standard product with zero defects? Can we help increase sales to the original market or extend them into adjacent markets? Can we help control variable costs that invariably inflate with volume? Can we help prepare for the first product proliferation that will extend the initial line?

Our answers will be the basis for our penetration of growth businesses.

A Business at Maturity

Finally, let us take a customer business that has become mature. Without knowing anything more, just that it is mature, we know what the manager's objective must be. He must ensure the competitiveness of his business by reducing its costs and increasing its productivity so that it can be among its industry's low-cost, high-efficiency producers. In a mature industry where commodity products have lost their differentiation and where the overall size of the market may not be expandable, low cost and increased cost-effectiveness are the only available strategies for margin protection.

What approach should we take? What is the first thing we should say? We must address the business life cycle. Since we know that cost control and productivity improvement are a mature manager's fixations, our dialog should focus on them. Can we help the manager reduce his labor content? Can we help reduce scrap and downtime? Can we help increase volume without increasing costs? Can we decrease costs? Can we add product value through marginal renovation? Can we increase market share at competitive expense?

Our answers will be the basis for our penetration of mature businesses.

Some of these points of departure for penetration are summarized in Figure 1-1, in correlation with the stage of the life cycle to which they relate. They are spelled out in greater detail in Figure 1-2.

Revealing "Our Game"

Our life-cycle dialog will reveal what we are good at, what "our game" is. We will discover that we are good at getting new businesses out of the starting gate on budget and on time or we are good at keeping mature, commodity-type businesses competitive. Or we may be able to say, We are good across the board. We can start to partner a customer business in startup and grow with it throughout its life cycle, accelerating its growth along the way and postponing maturity.

In addition, our dialogs will reveal our position in the market. Do customers come to us when they are starting up

Figure 1-2. **Life-cycle business opportunity compendium.**

Startup

#1 Priority objective: Achieve market entry on time
Needs to Achieve Priority Objective

1. Market database of target market niche
2. Forecast
3. Product plan and production schedule
4. Sales and distribution plan
5. Product and manufacturing process design
6. Product quality assurance
7. Beta testing, clinical trials
8. Inventory control

Entry

#1 Priority objective: Get product out the door
Needs to Achieve Priority Objective

1. Rescale for volume production
2. Refinement of product design and process and facility design
3. Quality control
4. Order entry, billing, and receivables collection systems
5. Customer service
6. Market database correction
7. Inventory mix control

Growth

#1 Priority objective: Fulfill market opportunity and avoid opportunity loss
Needs to Achieve Priority Objective

1. Quality standardization
2. Higher rate of volume, market share, and profits

Figure 1-2. **(continued)**

___

  3. Customer service
  4. Sales financing
  5. Sales force automation
  6. Inventory mix control
  7. Financial controls
  8. Startup of next product

Maturity

#1 Priority objective: Keep business going at highest
margins
Needs to Achieve Priority Objective

  1. Cost containment and reduction
  2. Productivity improvement
  3. Cash flow insurance
  4. Make-or-buy decisions in favor of "buy" (Strate-
    gic alliances)
  5. Inventory mix control
  6. Maintenance management
  7. New-product proliferation
  8. New-business diversification

___

new business? Or do they come when they are in troubled maturity? Where is our sales initiative concentrated? Are we actively promoting ourselves as new-business growers or productivity improvers for mature businesses? Do we improve customer profits primarily through sales development or cost reduction? Are most of our customers in a growth phase or are they mature? Did this concentration simply happen or did we plan it this way?

No matter what phases of customer life cycles we affect, an important question is whether we affect the most critical events in each phase. This is where the money is. At startup, do we make sure the entire business is being driven by its most likely market? At entry, can we standardize and upscale the startup business for volume? In growth, can we help fulfill the complete market opportunity offered to the business and avoid the opportunity loss from leaving attainable profits on the table? In maturity, can we maintain margins for a customer's business or regenerate its growth?

It is not enough to say, Yes we can do these things. We must be able to say, We do these things *best*. Only in that way can we become the industry standard for getting startups to entry or entrants into growth or mature businesses into regrowth.

When we can prove that nobody does it better, penetration strategy based on customer life cycles will have its ultimate payoff: Our own life cycle will always be in growth.

The life-cycle stages we affect in our customers' businesses will tell us what kind of supplier we are. If we affect customers' businesses in their growth phases, we will be an entrepreneurial business whose capabilities will focus on new products and getting them out the customer's door. We will be principally a sales developer. If we are a technology-based supplier, we will concentrate on assuring the cost, quality, and continuity of product design and manufacture. If we are a marketing-based supplier, we will concentrate on assuring sales. The more mature we are, the more we will devote our capabilities to cost avoidance and reduction in both our customer business and in our own. If we primarily affect customer businesses in their mature phase, we will be chiefly cost sensitive and secondarily concerned with maintaining or increasing market share for our customers.

A customer's life cycle abounds in opportunity for us to add value. At some stages, the principal value we can add will be through the avoidance or reduction, even the elimination, of costs. At other stages, we will have to increase productivity or sales to add value. At still other stages, we can do both. In every case, the end results will be the same. We will have improved a customer's profits in ways that he cannot do himself or that no one else can do as well.

Can We Help?

When a customer business is in the growth phases of its life cycle, it needs to maximize productivity and sales. Can we help? If so, we can penetrate with our products, services, or systems. As a customer business matures, it needs to minimize the costs of its asset base, increase productivity as well as win or win back market share. Can we help? If so, we can penetrate. There is no mystery about it. We can penetrate because our added values will precisely meet and match the needs of our customers.

The knowledge of the values that our customers need at each stage of their life cycle and of the values that we can add to them becomes our most precious penetration resource. Its importance supersedes our products. Our values become the drive forces for our penetration, not just for getting into business with our customers but penetrating again and again into successive opportunities.

If the customer's business is new, we can help improve his profits in the startup, entry, and growth phases of the life cycle. We must know in advance the problems in each life-cycle phase that we can help avoid or reduce and the opportunities we can help capitalize. We must know what solutions work best. We must know how to implement them most cost-effectively in the customer's business. We must know how much value to expect from them and when the value can be brought down to the customer's bottom line. If the customer's business is mature, we must know the same things about the mature phase of the customer's life cycle. Whenever we penetrate, we must be able to partner with the customer as if the two of us are jointly starting or growing a new business or regrowing a mature one.

Before we attempt penetration, we must know the critical few events in the customer's business that we can—that we must—sell into. These are the same critical events that the customer himself must manage, either as costs to be controlled or productivity and sales to be expanded, at that particular phase of his growth cycle. Thus, we and our customer will have from the outset the single most important characteristic of partners: common objectives. When objectives are same-same, then and only then can profitmaking be win-win.

We can ask our customer, Are you starting up a new business? We can help you achieve market entry sooner and more cost-effectively. Are you already in entry? We can help you achieve growth. Are you presently growing? We can help you continue to grow. Has your growth already slowed in maturity? We can help you become recompetitive through new growth.

Prequalifying Customer Needs

By knowing the customer's life-cycle phase, we automatically know the customer's needs; they are prequalified. We know how prospective the customer is for our products, services, and systems; we know where their application will do the most good and approximately how much good they can do. We know the customer decision-makers we must call on and the charges being imposed on them to cut costs and boost productivity and sales.

As a partner, we will never lack for penetration opportunities into a customer. Nor will we lack something to sell or someone to sell it to. Getting in will vanish as a problem. Getting upstairs to sell will vanish with it, since business function decision-makers—our natural partners—are always upstairs. Once in, getting beaten out on price will no longer be a problem either. No temporarily lowered price can ever be cheap enough to outvalue a partner's continuing contribution to customer profit.

What must we know to penetrate customers as their partner?

We must know the phases of customer life cycles that we can best affect. We must know how to affect them and by how much we can improve their contributions to cost or productivity or sales. We must know how to partner with their decision-makers as the expert counsel in their particular phase of business life.

When we have learned how to penetrate as a partner, we will never have to buy or sell our way in again. We will be able to assess the price we have been paying—literally—to be a vendor: the price in lowered margins and higher sales costs, the price in low-level customer contacts, the price of ignorance of customer business facts and growth plans, and the price of perpetual vulnerability to competition. These reasons are sufficient by themselves to alter our penetration strategy. But there is one more reason that will confirm our partnership. Once our customers learn how we can improve their profits as their partner, they will never *let* us buy or sell our way in again.

Knowing Our Value

If we can help new customer businesses improve and accelerate their growth, making them grow bigger or faster than they could otherwise, we will have highly profitable customers. As a result, we will be highly profitable ourselves. Our next greatest profit potential after new-business growth will come from helping mature customer businesses improve profits by increasing their sales volume. If we can affect customer businesses in both of these life-cycle phases, we can bring mega-profits to ourselves and our customers.

If we do not know where in the customer's life cycle we make our greatest impact, we cannot know how much our impact can be. If we do not know how much our impact can be, we cannot know its value. If we do not know its added value to the customer, we cannot partner with him as a value-adder. Nor can we have a value-based foundation for our price.

Partnerships are value-based. A partner is known by the value he brings. Maximum value-bringers make the most preferred partners. Who needs minimum values? A supplier partner trades on his added value. He can say, I know your business. You are a startup. I know where a startup's main costs are concentrated. I can help you avoid some of them and reduce others. As a result of my partnering with your startup managers, their cost of gaining market entry will be reduced by an average $500,000. In addition, their certainty of entry will be increased by an average 90 percent.

Now the customer can compute the supplier partner's value. The customer knows the value of an additional $500,000. He knows what he will invest it in and what return he can expect. In this way, he fixes its value. He also knows the value of added confidence provided by an enhanced certainty of market entry for his startup. He will not be able to quantify it precisely. But it makes the $500,000 a firmer number to plan on. And it makes his planned payback from entry more assured, in both its amount and its timing. These are the values that a good supplier partner provides.

The customer can say, My partner means the return on an added $500,000 to me this year. Even more, he represents an increased certainty of achieving some of my other immediate objectives as well. By assuring them, or maybe even helping me achieve them sooner, that could be worth another half a million dollars. So my partner really means the return on a million dollars to me this year—my million-dollar partner.

In a world where most suppliers are known to their customers by the most recent reduction in price they can be induced to offer, being known by the most recent improvement in profits is the epitome of meaningful differentiation.

What price offer can compete against it?

Two As-If Scenarios

Let us create two as-if scenarios to see how partnered penetration works. First, we will act as if we were penetrating a new business. Then we will act as if we were penetrating a mature business.

New-Business Penetration

In our as-if approach to a new business, we will enter it through the manufacturing function. We will be selling a computerized factory automation system that provides computer-aided design, manufacturing, and engineering information and control.

We can say, We have been studying your business. We see that you are in the startup phase of a new manufacturing venture that represents a diversification of your mainstream business. The startup phase of a new business is an area of our expertise. We are good at helping manufacturing managers like you avoid predictable problems before they can occur or solve them quickly if they do. We know the major cost contributors of startup: process and product control in your pilot operations, standardizing quality as close as possible to the zero-defects level to minimize scrap and recall, building in productivity, and building out downtime—all the while keeping within budget and making market entry on time. We have a lot of experience in these areas with high-speed, high-volume operations.

We have put our experience into the form of three new-business models, beginning with startup where you are now and continuing through entry and growth. Each model shows the normal range of costs we are used to finding in the key areas of our customers' operations that we affect and the average amounts by which we are able to reduce them or avoid them entirely. We would also like to show you the average impact we have been able to make on increasing sales through quality assurance and reduction of downtime. How do your costs compare to our norms? What would the value be to you of reducing your costs to our averages, and thereby improving your profits?

Mature-Business Penetration

In our as-if approach to a mature business, we will take a different tack to show the flexibility of driving sales from the customer's life cycle. Our entry point will be marketing, not manufacturing, and we will be selling a service rather than a factory automation system.

We can say, We have been studying your business. We see that you are in a fiercely competitive market where product differentiation is no longer possible by exclusive performance benefits but only through price. The mature phase of main-stream, long-established breadwinner businesses is an area of our expertise. We are good at helping marketing managers like you reduce the cost of incremental sales and increasing profits from sales at the same time, all without adding further cost to your asset base. We know how to increase profit share without expanding your sales force, without adding to your advertising budget, or without reducing price.

We have put our experience into the form of a mature-business model. The model shows the average impact each of our sales development strategies can make on volume and profits. How do your marketing investments compare to our norms? What would the value be to you of reallocating them to improve your profits according to our averages?

Specializing in "the Customer's Business"

Penetrating our customers through the opportunity windows in their business life cycles teaches us the partial wisdom of what has been called the mightiest maxim of marketing: to know our customer's business. No such entity as *the* custom-er's business exists. There is *the customer's business at startup* or *the customer's business at entry* or *the customer's business in growth or maturity*. Each is a different business. It may make the same products, derive its capabilities from the same func-tions, and even be led by the same managers. But each stage of its life cycle offers us a different penetration opportunity. For this reason, we must regard it as a different business. Our pen-etration strategy must be geared to the difference.

Depending on the nature of our business, we may be able to affect customer businesses at one, two, three, or all four of their life-cycle stages. But this will be a concern mostly to us alone. Our customers will want to know only one thing. If they are in startup, they will want to partner with a supplier who is a specialist in startups. If they are in entry or growth or maturity, they will be similarly dedicated to partnering with a supplier who is dedicated to solving the specific types of cost problems they face at their stage of the business life cycle or to helping them fulfill their specific types of sales opportunities. Our other capabilities will be extraneous.

Penetration through our customers' life cycles demands that we be specialists in their stages of commercial life. We can, of course, be specialists in several stages. But each customer will care only about the one he is in. Are we experts in moving him out of it, as with startup and entry and some forms of maturity? Are we experts in helping him perpetuate his position, as with other forms of maturity and with growth? Nothing else will matter.

What does it mean to be a specialist in improving the profit contribution of a startup business, for example? How can we prove that we fill the bill? A specialist is dedicated to improving profits for specific types of customers, in this case customers who are starting up a new business venture. It does not necessarily mean that the specialist focuses on a specific product line, such as computers. Nor does it mean that the specialist concentrates only on a specific customer process, such as manufacturing. Specialists in applying computers to customer manufacturing processes are vendors, not partners; they penetrate through the purchasing function on the basis of price and performance. In order to penetrate as a partner, we must be specialists in something else—the ability to improve profits at a customer's particular stage in his life cycle.

The specialist in computers does not automatically improve his customers' profits by selling them his computers. He may simply add to their costs. The specialist in manufacturing applications of computers does not automatically improve his customers' profits either. He may add to their costs even more. The only way we can prove that we add value to customer profits is to make profit dollars our product and then demonstrate how much of them we can add to each customer. If we are verifiable experts in our specialty, we will have financial models that can prove our contributions. These models will be our stock in trade. They, not our products or services, will be our prime penetration tools.

Each model will act as the standard of profit improvement for the customer's type of business at its specific stage of the life cycle. For startups in each industry to which we are dedicated, we will be the owners of the standard industry model of enhanced profit contribution by startups. We will have a similar capability for entrants or growth businesses or mature businesses. Our models will contain the industry norms for costs, productivity, and sales. By partnering with us, each customer will be better able to approach, or exceed, the norms. That is the benefit of engaging our expertise as specialists.

Investing in the Hot Spots

Penetrating through a customer's life cycle is penetrating where the opportunities are. We can be sure the opportunities are there because the needs are there. Every startup business needs entry. Every entry business needs growth. Every growth business needs the perpetuation of its growth. Every mature business needs to have its margins maintained or re-grown. There are no ifs, and, or buts about these needs. They are eternal foundations for our business as a supplier, as long as we can supply the values that will benefit our customers' needs.

We will always be in the right place at the right time with the right product. It will not matter if our customer's industry is down. We can help them grow faster than the industry. It does not matter if our own industry is in a slump, its volume depressed and its products reduced to undifferentiated commodities. If we can find the way to convert our product values to profit values for our customers, we can differentiate ourselves and penetrate customer businesses where the need for our values is greatest. No customer, however saturated with products like ours or however cost-constrained, can afford to turn us away.

How can we be so sure? Logic supplies the answer. Life-cycle penetration works for us because we are offering to add value to precisely the same problems and opportunities that our customers have valued as their topmost priorities. Their priorities are dictated to them, as they are to us, by the position of their businesses in the life cycle. So we know in advance where the "hot buttons" are in each customer's business—the cost problems he must control and the productivity and sales opportunities he must increase if he is to reach his business objectives. We do not have to grope blindly through his business in search of something to bid on. Nor do we need to sit passively by, waiting for him to request a proposal from us. On our own initiative, we can zero in on the selfsame targets where our customer has planned to allocate his own resources. We know where his investments are going. Our task is to become one of them. The way we do that is to prove the superiority of our return.

Customers cannot tell us there is no money to put against our mutual objective. There is—because they *must* achieve it, with or without us. Customers cannot tell us that the objective is not a priority right now. It is, if the business is to succeed—and, in some instances, survive. Customers cannot tell us that they will take our penetration proposals under advisement for contemplation and deliberation. The incremental profits we propose are too vital, their time value too pressing to permit delay.

The relationship we have with our customers will undergo significant change. They will not be looking for reasons to postpone purchase. They will be looking for ways to accelerate their profits. How can we become one of them?

We must become a preferred source of return for our customers on their investments. Their money is going to go somewhere. It can go internally, where it will be invested in-house with staff services. Or it can go outside to a supplier. How can we direct it our way? The case we make for ourselves as a prime investment opportunity depends on the return for the investment that we can propose. We must be a better bet, better than alternative claimants for the same investment on the basis of one or more of the three specifications that determine the "goodness" of return:

1. We must supply a greater return for the same investment or the same return for a smaller investment.
2. We must start our return sooner or have it peak earlier than competitive investments.
3. We must offer greater confidence that we will deliver the return we promise when we promise it.

Combining Comfort and Urgency

Customers "do deals"—whether they involve making purchase decisions or making investments for the highest or fastest or surest return—at the same point in their decision-making process. It is the point where their two main criteria come together, *comfort* and *urgency*. If we are going to penetrate with the shortest possible sales cycle, our mission must be to combine comfort and urgency quickly.

A customer will partner with us when he has enough comfort that we are specialists in improving the profits of his kind of business and when he has enough urgency to get his hands on the improved profits without incurring any additional opportunity loss.

We must be prepared to enter every initial penetration *without* sufficient customer comfort or urgency. The only safe assumption is that all new customers will be uncomfortable with us, not only because customers are traditionally defensive with suppliers but also because they are uncertain in dealing with suppliers who propose to partner with them instead of vend. Let us expect, at worst, discomfort instead of comfort or, at best, insufficient comfort to close with us. Our first penetration hurdle is to create comfort. How can we do this? The only workable approach is to prove compliance with the third specification of the "goodness" of return: that we will deliver the amount of return we promise when we promise it.

Let us also expect a lack of urgency by a new customer to invest his money with us. Why should he rush to investment? All customers are prudent investors, wise in trading off among competing opportunities and skilled in performing due diligence in scoping them out. So our second penetration hurdle is to create urgency. How can we do this? The only workable approach is to prove compliance with the second specification: that we will start our return sooner so that every day the customer delays costs him money. In this way, we must make the customer uncomfortable for *not* partnering. When it is more comfortable to partner because it is more profitable, at that moment we will penetrate.

2

Targeting the Customer

Deriving Sales Strategy from the Customer's Life Cycle

A small customer may have a single business. In that case, the nature of the business will be determined by stage of the business life cycle. If it is in growth, the customer will be a growth company; if the business is mature, the customer will be mature.

A large customer will have several businesses, each at its own stage of the life cycle. The mainstream business—the cash cow that provides the major contribution of revenues—will probably be mature. One or two smaller businesses may be in startup. If the customer is lucky, at least one other business will be in growth.

While all these businesses belong to the same customer, each is a different business. Their mix of needs, and the priorities assigned to them, are different. Their objectives are different and so are their strategies. Different, too, is their culture. Startups, for example, are generally less formal, more venturesome, and wholly dedicated to sales. Getting to the top-level decision-makers is easy, going through channels is swift and decisive, and the ability to move fast is vital. Mature businesses, on the other hand, are more ponderous and political. Cost control may be more important than sales, decision-making influencers may be obscure or unknown, and the opportunity for a supplier to prove his value may be constrained by ponderous negotiation.

All these factors will be considerations in our penetration strategy. They will, in fact, determine it. We would not try to penetrate a startup business by offering cost-control benefits that were unrelated to the company's prime "hot button"—sales. Nor, conversely, would we try to penetrate a mature business by offering sales-revenue benefits that were unrelated to the "hot button" of cost control.

Guided by the life-cycle stage of each business, we would, in sum, "make the blandishment fit the time." In doing so, the life-cycle needs of *each customer business* would become our specific targets for penetration.

When we make a customer's life-cycle needs our penetration targets, we are defining the business life cycle as a needs cycle. At each of the cycle's four critical stages, we are saying two things about customer needs: they are predetermined by the life-cycle stage and therefore *predictable* by us, and they are *different* enough at each stage to require that we become a specialist in the stages we want to penetrate.

Because they are predictable, we can gear up to penetrate life-cycle needs on the basis of our investment being returnable. And because they are different at each stage, we can become expert in the stages to which we can add the greatest profits. Our success in penetration will be in direct proportion to our positioning as a specialist.

Time-Determined Targets

Each life-cycle stage of a customer business is time-determined. Except for maturity, each stage represents a milestone to be achieved as quickly as possible. Delay is the enemy. First of all, delay adds cost. The longer a business stays in startup, the longer entry is deferred; the slower that growth takes place, the greater the investment that must be sunk and the more remote will be the accumulation of earnings. Delay adds uncertainty. It provides time for competition to mobilize or become entrenched, technology to be preempted, and market needs to shift. Delay also erodes patience. While waiting for payback or profit, management may grow restless, lose its enthusiasm, and find alternate investment opportunities that appear to be more attractive. If it pulls the plug, a potentially profitable business may be lost.

Reaching each milestone on time is crucial. Arriving ahead of time is money in the bank. Missing a milestone prejudices each successive event that depends on it. Achieving a milestone, however, guarantees nothing except the opportunity to try to reach the next one.

The drive in the first two stages is to break through to the next event. The focus of startup is to enter. The focus of entry is to reach breakeven so that growth can begin. The focus of growth, however, is to keep setting new high rates of profitmaking for as long as possible.

Our role with customers is therefore clear. At a customer's startup, how much faster can we help achieve entry; how much more surely? At entry, how much faster can we help achieve first sales; how much more surely? In growth, how much faster can we help growth occur, how much longer can we help maintain high rates of growth, and how much more surely? And in regrowth after maturity, how much faster and more economically can we help growth recur, how much longer can we help maintain growth, and how much more surely?

All these basic questions break down into many specific questions, each of them pregnant with sales opportunity. Can startup be shortened so that entry can be accelerated, even by a single day? We may be able to make this happen by assuring the quality of the customer's initial product. Can growth be accelerated by condensing breakeven, if only by a single day? We may be able to make this happen by maximizing uptime of the customer's production process, minimizing inventory, or optimizing the billing and collection cycle.

Can regrowth in maturity be accelerated by reducing

costs, improving productivity, and making cash management more professional? We may be able to make this happen. If so, we can help turn a declining customer into a growing customer whose profitmaking rate will be born again.

Target-Determined Opportunities

Customers are rightfully regarded as markets. But this is a gross definition. A more finite definition, and therefore more practical, is to regard a customer's life-cycle events as our markets. This is where our opportunity to grow customers will be found. Each event invites growth. Indeed, growth is what each event is all about. The startup business of a customer wants to grow to be an entrant. The entrant business wants to grow to be a big winner. The big-winner business wants to continue to grow, and the mature customer may want to regrow to become a winner again.

The stages of a customer life cycle predetermine our opportunity. Will we be a grower of startup business, accelerating their passage into entry and growth? Or will we be a regrower of mature businesses? Will we be able to enjoy the best of both worlds and be grower and regrower alike?

Based on our capabilities, our work will be cut out for us. Our customers are always starting up, entering, growing, or regrowing. They are always seeking acceleration of their rate of earnings growth. As a result, we never lack the opportunity for useful work. We are not constrained by waiting for requests for proposals. Nor is our chance for improved profit growth limited by competitive bids. The initiative in penetration through a customer's life cycle is ours and ours alone.

To open a penetration window, we need simply to address one of our customers' businesses through its stage of the life cycle. Life-cycle stages will be our entry points. "We specialize in improving the profit contribution of new businesses in your industry," we can say to a customer. "We know how to keep a startup on budget, how to make sure it has segmented its market properly, and how to build reliability into its first product.

We know how to help ensure first sales, increase productivity to keep it parallel with demand, yet control quality and inventory at the same time. We know how to help expand market share, extend the original product line, create alternate channels of distribution, and still exceed the industry average on the collection of receivables."

How is one of the two things we must know best. *How much* is the other: How much improvement we can make to the profit contribution of a customer's business operations by the value we add to them. We will be known by the value we add. Unless we know our value, we cannot claim to be a specialist. Unless our customers also know our value, we cannot claim the specialist's premium price.

Do we know our value? The answer to this question separates the specialist from the vendor, who knows only his cost. If we fixate on our cost, we will seek to transfer it to our customers. We will base our price on it. We will justify our price by comparing our product's quality and performance—the results of our costs—to competition. We will force customers to choose the lowest cost. As a result, we will receive the lowest price.

If we know our value, we can seek to add it to our customers. We can base our price on it. We can relate our price to our value so that price is seen as an investment and our value is its return. We can position ourselves as representing the highest value. As a result, we can receive the highest price.

If we can consistently deliver the highest value, our value will become perceived by our customers as their "industry standard of value." All competing values will be unsuccessfully compared against our value. If they are found to be wanting, we will be found to be incomparable.

The Critical Success Factors

Each life-cycle stage has its critical success factors. They are always few. Their achievement is therefore crucial. If the critical factors are botched or bungled, the customer's business objective will suffer disproportionately. This is because the critical factors are multipliers. They multiply the customer's chance of success. On the downside, they multiply the certainty and swiftness of failure.

If the few critical factors are managed well, the many noncritical factors can be dealt with less than well and the business will still grow. Conversely, attending to all the noncritical factors at the expense of the few critical factors can foredoom a customer's growth.

As we prospect for penetration opportunity, we must drive our prospecting from the critical success factors in our customer businesses. They will be our opportunity windows: the most heightened customer needs that we can serve. How can we make them work for us?

Our prospecting should follow a five-step sequence:

1. Select the life-cycle model that represents the customer's business mode.
2. Use the model of the business mode to select a customer function that is essential for profitmaking.
3. Study the function to choose one of its critical success factors where an important cost can be reduced or an important opportunity to increase productivity or sales can be seized.
4. Partner the decision-maker who is responsible for reducing the cost or increasing productivity or sales.
5. Propose an incrementally improved profit based on reducing the cost or increasing productivity or sales.

Selecting the customer's life-cycle mode begins the penetration process. But penetration occurs only when a proposal to improve the profit of the customer's business is implemented. This makes penetration a good deal more than simply standing before a decision-maker. Driving a business from the customer means that penetration requires adding to his bottom line. This tells us what it is that must be penetrated: not the customers' decision-making or operating processes but his economic process. Either we penetrate by entry into a customer's financial condition or we will be merely tangential to it, striking it a glancing blow but making no measurably significant impact.

To capitalize fully on the opportunities that we will discover by prospecting according to the five-step sequence, we must follow three rules.

1. We must *concentrate* on each market we have segmented.
2. We must *customize* each solution for each customer in each of our markets.
3. We must *consult* to each customer on the most cost-effective application of each solution.

Concentrating on a Single Market

We will qualify as a specialist in our customer business only by specializing in improving the profits of his specific industry. More than one industry qualifies the generalist; generalists sell something to everybody. Specialists improve the profits of the customers they select as their specialty. This is a significant difference. By contrast, a generalist's customers do the choosing: they select him from among alternate vendors.

In this way, specialists control their businesses. They are in charge of their sources of funds—their customers—aggressively cultivating them and maximizing the contribution they make. They do not wait for markets to mobilize; they mobilize them. Out of all the businesses in this market, they say to the customers they select to grow, We have chosen to help you grow. From this moment on, your growth will become our mutual objective. We will plan it together. Together we will implement our plan. The plan will interlock our growth.

The specialist commits all his eggs to his market basket. His customers can simultaneously be grown by several specialists, each of whom makes his impact on different functions of a customer's business. But the specialist cannot take refuge in diversity. His strength is quite the opposite; it lies in concentration.

It has been said that a generalist knows a little about a lot; the specialist, by contrast, knows a lot about a little. To say the same thing in a different way, the specialist knows everything about something instead of something about everything. The specialist's "something" is the market whose profits he improves. He knows the customer operations that he affects. He knows their normal contributions to costs, productivity, and sales. He knows the values he can add to these norms. He knows how to add them, how to measure them, and how to prove them. His values are the authoritative standards for all customers in the industry of his specialty. Customers who want to achieve the standard or, having achieved it, want to maintain or exceed it, turn to the specialist. Where else would they go?

Since the specialist sinks or swims on his choice of each industry he selects to grow, his selection criteria must be unerring. What should he look for? Fortunately, there are only two checkpoints. Each market he chooses for penetration must either be one that he is growing right now or one he believes he can grow. How can he tell? Each market's growth potential must be based on reducing costs that he is expert in reducing or improving productivity or sales in ways that he is expert in stimulating.

When we concentrate our business on a specific market, two things become apparent. A market is homogeneous: All customers in the same market have similar needs. Customers, however, are heterogeneous: Each customer is different in the way his needs are valued and in the values by which they must be solved.

An industry's norms act as an envelope into which we can put our knowledge of the competitive context in which a customer does business. We can put two kinds of information in the envelope. One is the industry's working-capital situation. The other is its operating ratios.

By analyzing an industry's working-capital norms, we

can see how cash flows in the industry. How many times a year does capital turn over? How long does it normally take to collect receivables? What is the percentage rate of inventory turn? When we know these norms, we can trend them against years past to see if business in the industry is growing or slowing down—in other words, to see where the industry stands in its life cycle.

When we learn our customer's norms for each of these categories, we can match them against his industry norms to see if he is ahead of or behind average industry performance.

The second kind of industry information that must go into our envelope is operating ratios. Each industry has its own critical set of ratios that tell how cost-effectively it is operating. Operating ratios tell an industry how efficiently it is converting resources into dollars. Depending on the industry, we may want to know how much it nets for each unit it sells, what its average gross margin is, how much it costs to make an average sale, and how much profit each sale earns. When we know these norms, we can trend them against years past to see if businesses in the industry are making more or less money and are spending more or less to do it—in other words, to see how well the industry is being managed.

When we learn our customer's norms for each of these categories, we can match them against his industry norms to see if he is ahead of or behind average industry performance.

Figure 2-1 shows a situation survey for keeping track of comparative working-capital and operating ratios for both our customer and his industry.

A knowledge of customer industry norms is the *sine qua non* of penetration. Without them, there can be no pretension of being the industry specialist. With them, we can take the first step in penetration. We can say to a customer, We know your industry. That is exactly one-half of the penetration equation. The second half is being able to say, We know your business and how it departs from your industry's norms. Unless we can take the second step, we will have made a long run for a short slide.

Figure 2-1. Situation survey: Industry and customer norms.

	Customer Industry Norm	% +/− Year Ago	Customer Norm	% +/− Year Ago	+/− Customer Deviation from Industry Norm
Working Capital					
Amount of working capital (current assets − current liabilities)	___	___	___	___	___
Number of times per year receivables turn over (net sales ÷ average customer receivables)	___	___	___	___	___
Number of days per collection period (365 ÷ number of times per year receivables turn)	___	___	___	___	___
Percent inventory turnover (cost of goods sold ÷ end-year inventory)	___	___	___	___	___

Operating Ratios	Customer Industry Norm	% +/- Year Ago	Customer Norm	% +/- Year Ago	+/- Customer Deviation from Industry Norm
Net income per unit					
Percent gross profit (margin)					
Percent net profit to net sales					
Costs as percent of sales					
Costs as percent of their cost group (contribution)					
Percent sales expense to sales (cost of sales: investment to revenue)					

Customizing Each Solution

Since our customers live in what is to them the only real world, that of their own customized values, we must live in the same world with them. The only way we can do this is by offering customized solutions whose added values are prescriptive to their needs.

In order to penetrate a customer business through its life cycle, we must set forth a two-part proposition:

1. We own the industry model that shows the normal costs for the key operations of your type of business at its current stage of the life cycle.

2. Because your costs differ, we will customize our general solution to bring them closer to the norms in the most timely, cost-effective manner.

Premium value—the kind of value a customer needs to significantly restructure his costs or productivity or sales—can never be delivered by standard solutions. The true added value of a solution is not found in its performance enhancements but in the way we can custom fit it to each customer's operations. Custom fitting includes several benefits: How our solution is applied to the customer's business function where it must perform, how we train customer people in its operation and maintenance, how we upgrade our solution to keep it on the leading edge, and how we migrate it to affect other problems and opportunities within the customer's business.

When we penetrate with customized solutions, we do not enter a customer's business bearing product specification sheets, product catalogs or brochures, or even our products themselves. We need only to present two penetration tools. One is case-history testimonials that prove our capability to customize profit-improvement solutions that beat industry norms in similar processes in similar businesses in the customer's industry. The other is a customized cost-benefit analysis that proves on paper our capability to improve the profit contribution of the customer's own operation.

The cost-benefit analysis will show the specific costs and the specific benefits that will accrue to the customer's business. *The premium value that we can deliver, expressed as net profit and rate of return on investment, will be our solution.* It will be the basis for our penetration, our partnership, and our premium price.

Consulting to Each Customer

Customers live in a world of "if only." *If only* we could move faster, they say. If only we could do this or that less expensively. If only we could cut this cost here, overcome this delay there, be certain that we can limit our exposure by this amount, have our margins hold at this percent. Everything a customer plans or takes action on is done on an if-only basis. *If only* he could actually do these things, his profits would be improved.

What does a customer want to hear most, not just from his own people but from his suppliers as well? He wants to hear help. Help comes in the form of options. *What if* we do this? Here are the dollars that will most likely result. *What if* we do that? Here are the most likely dollars from that option. "What if" is the consultant's stock in trade. It is the correlate of the customer's "if only." Just as "if only" is a customer buying signal, "what if" is the consultant's proposal to sell.

Consultants and their customers communicate through mutual hypotheses. The customer poses a problem from the priorities on his wish list in the form of a distress signal. If there is a solution out there, the customer's hypothesis is that he will hear about it. The answer comes back in the form of a solution. If the customer is interested, the consultant's hypothesis is that the customer will ask the magic question: *How?* How can I get that solution?

This is the ritualistic mating dance of consultants and their customers. Customers send out a call asking what is available out there. Consultants respond by identifying themselves with their solutions. Each consultant proposes his solution in the form of *new profits* for his customer. This is the ultimate solution to all major customer problems since insufficient profits are always their ultimate cause. Consultants deal in ultimate solutions. For them, intermediate solutions such as improved cost-avoidance or improved productivity or improved sales are stepping stones to improved profits. Unless avoided costs can ultimately be converted into profits, what good are they? Unless added sales or productivity can ultimately translate into incremental dollars on the bottom line, why bother?

The consultant's hypothesis is always expressed in terms of, What if you can gain this amount of new profits? A consultant is known by the quality of his hypotheses. *How much* do they offer? *How soon* do they pay out? *How sure* is their realization? The ideal hypothesis pays out a significant number of new dollars quickly and surely. The worst hypothesis proposes significant profits with uncertainty. This makes them coveted but unreal, incapable of being acted on, and therefore worthless.

Consultants install products or services or systems but they sell the profits that their systems can produce in the customer's operations. The profits, not the systems, are their solutions. Alleged consultants get hung up on this fact. They call their systems "solutions." They attach a price to them and let their customers calculate their value. In this way, customers are forced to act as their own consultants. They pay themselves for it, too, deducting their "fee" from the price they pay for the would-be consultant's system.

Would-be consultants who vend systems under the guise of solutions can frequently be shown the falsity of their positioning with this question: Which are you getting paid for, the solution or the system? If they do not even know the value of the solution—the profits it improves for the customer—the answer becomes immediately clear. By being paid for the system, they are being compensated as vendors, not consultants. They are being paid not for the value they generate in a customer's business but for the costs they have generated in their own.

Penetration must be an exchange of values, not costs. A customer's current values must be traded up for improved values. The consultant's values must be traded up as well. His capabilities to improve customer profits have an inventory value on the shelf. Only when these capabilities are applied to a customer's operations can their shelf value be enhanced into a premium operating value for which the consultant can be paid a premium price.

Opening a Prospect

A consultant positions himself by his opener. His first words define his expertise and, thereby, his business. They tell what he is good at doing and with whom. They position the nature and the amount of his value to the customers he serves.

Customers who can benefit from the nature of the consultant's value, and to whom the amount of value he offers is significant, automatically qualify themselves as his prime prospects. Customers who can benefit the most qualify as the consultant's key accounts.

Consultants who are driven by their customers eschew vendorese, the language of vendors. In one way or another, through semantic subterfuge and linguistic legerdemain, vendorese speaks to customers in variations of its basic theme: "Have I got a *product* for you." Sometimes vendors substitute *system* for product; other times, they use the word *solution*. For the vendor, nothing happens until he moves a product. Nothing much happens afterward, either.

The consultant is driven by the same two basic needs that drive his customer. One is the need to control costs, avoiding new costs wherever possible and reducing current costs everywhere. At the same time, because no business grows by cost reduction alone, the customer needs to raise his productivity and the profits he makes on sales. All customer needs can be put into these two general categories. This is because they are the categories of moneymaking. Costs set forth a customer's investment in his business; profits enumerate his return.

Based on what a customer's business is all about—profits—a consultant knows what he must be about. He must be a reducer of his customer's costs that he can affect. He must also be an increaser of his customer's productivity and profitable sales volume. Once he knows what he is about, he can relate it to what his customer is about. This gives him his opener.

At this point in the life cycle of your business, a consultant says by way of introducing himself, I know the business functions on which you must rely the most. I know where the main costs cluster in each function. I know what they average in other businesses similar to your own. If I can learn your costs, I can compare them to your industry averages. If you are higher than average, I can help you come down. If you are already below the average, I can help you stay low or become even lower.

I know the productivity averages in business functions like yours. If you are below the average, I can help you improve output by reducing downtime, reducing scrap, and reducing defects that lead to recall. If you are above average, I can help you stay high or become even higher.

I know average prices in businesses like yours. I know the averages for margins and shares of market. I can help you retain share or build it, protect your margins or grow them, maintain price or raise it.

Tyro consultants pause here and ask their customers to take a function, any function, where an improved contribution to profit would be meaningful. Professional consultants come prepared with their own suggestions. They have already scoped their customer's business. They know where they can begin. They know by how much they can help. They know how soon their help will start to flow. This is where they enter—with the number of dollars they can add to the customer's business. This number is the end point of their calculations. But it is the starting point of their customer penetration.

Zeroing in on the Targets

To be able to scope penetration opportunity throughout our customer life cycles, we must know three things:

1. The current values in the customer operations that we can affect—the dollar values of a customer's current costs, current productivity levels, and current sales.
2. The prospective dollar values that we can add to customer operations.
3. The worth of our added dollar values to each customer operation.

Knowing Current Values

All customer operations are cost centers. Only one, the sales function, can be a profit center, and then only if profits from sales exceed the cost of sales. Customers have a choice of three strategies for managing their operations. One is to avoid or reduce costs while maintaining productivity. Another is to increase productivity while maintaining, reducing, or even increasing costs. The third is to eliminate an operation altogether, either spinning it out as an independent profit center to remove it from the corporate books or buying its output from an outside source instead of making it.

To penetrate a customer, we must be expert in his operations that we can affect by partnering with him in one or more of the strategies at his disposal. This means that we must have three kinds of smarts. We must be *process smart*—knowledgeable in the flow of the customer's process and the points where the critical costs cluster. We must be *applications smart*—knowledgeable in applying our product to the customer's process so that its contribution to cost can be reduced or its productivity can be increased. And we must be *validation smart*—knowledgeable in ways to quantify our contribution.

Knowing the customer's business takes all three types of smarts. In the areas of our expertise, we must know how a customer's process flows. We must be able to chart it from start to finish. We must know the 20 percent of its crunch points that contribute up to 80 percent of its costs. We must know the value of these costs. We must know the normal costs of these operations and the amount by which the customer's costs deviate from them. We must know how to bring the customer's costs closer to the norm if they exceed it or keep them below it if the customer is doing better than the norm. We must know by how much we can do this and how soon. When we know all these things, then we can say that we know the customer's business as far as the operations we affect are concerned. Anything less is vending.

Knowing Prospective Values

Vendors like to say that they are value-adders. Yet all they can usually quantify is the value of the cost they add when a customer buys from them. Rarely, if ever, do they know the value of the costs they reduce or the productivity or sales they increase inside a customer business. Yet this is every seller's most crucial value. Unless we know it, we are selling blind.

Even worse, we are selling product. If we do not know the value we add to the customer, we must sell what we know: our product's cost and its justification. As soon as we sell cost, we will come under the control of the customer's purchasing function whose primary purpose is cost control. We will be imprisoned in vending.

Added value does not take place at the factory. It takes place in the customer's business. All value is customer value. If we are going to add to a customer's value, we must first know what it is without our addition. This is the customer's "before." The new value will be the customer's "after." The difference between before and after is the *value added by our business*. In truth, it *is* our business. It is what we do and why we do it.

For the purposes of penetration, the value we add must become the product we sell. We must become a value-added seller. This means that we must know our product: the value that we represent.

In common with all products, value has its own specifications, which determine its performance capability—what it is able to do inside the customer's business. Our value's performance capability is customer-dependent. It will vary for each customer application. Each of our "products" will be unique to its customer. Except by chance, no two values will be the same.

Value has three specifications:

1. It has quantity. We will be able to add a lot of value or only a little.
2. It has time. We will be able to add value quickly or not for a while.
3. It has certainty. We will be able to add value with a high degree of certainty or we will hedge.

A mix of those three values are the benefits we will be able to offer to each customer. We must be able to quantify each one. If all we can say is, We are pretty sure that we can provide a lot of value to your operation rather soon, we will be saying nothing. Once we have quantified our value, then we will be able to learn our most important sales tool: what our added value is worth to our customer.

Knowing the Worth of Added Values

If we are able to offer our customer the added value of $1 as the result of doing business with us, what are we really offering him? The dollar has three values. One is its money value: A dollar is a dollar. Another is its time value: A dollar today is worth more than the same dollar tomorrow. Finally, the dollar has investment value: It can be invested at a rate of return that will multiply its original value severalfold.

Our value is worth what a customer can do with it. It is a function of how much he gets from us, when he gets it, and what he does with it. This is the ultimate worth of our dollar. Like value, worth occurs only in a customer's business. In order to create new worth for a customer, we must therefore get into the customer's business—into his operations, his processes, and his business functions—and work in partnership with him to make worth happen. We cannot create worth without him. Nor can he achieve the added worth we offer without us. To magnify the worth of a business, we and our customers need each other. This congruence of need makes us natural partners.

When we know what our value is worth to a customer, we and our customer can tell what kind of partner material we represent. If our value is the same as the customer can obtain working alone without us, we are not partner material. If our value is worth more than the customer can obtain working alone or with any other supplier, we are prime partner material. Anything less than that will be vending under false pretenses.

If we want to be a customer's prime partner, we must offer him the prime value. Nobody must be able to offer him better value specifications—either as much value or as soon or as sure. If we can achieve this position, our value will become the industry standard. Not only will we deliver the greatest value, but our value will be worth the most to our customers.

When that happens, we will have a new basis for price. No longer will our price need to reflect cost or competitive market value. Now we can relate our price to the worth of our value on a return-on-investment basis. The customer's added worth becomes his return. Our price becomes his investment. A premium return to the customer is his justification for making a premium investment in us.

This is the way specialist pricing transcends competitive bidding. Competition is no longer the index of price. Nor is cost. The true criterion of price shifts to customer value; all other bases for price are irrelevant. A competitor's lower price is no guarantee of his higher value. Nor does it warrant an assumption of greater worth to the customer. Under this approach to value-based pricing, a competitor could give his product away and it could still not guarantee the best customer value. A customer who has been taught to think this way by us would know this and not accept the competing product, free though it might be. What would his reason be? *He could not afford it.*

Modeling Added Values

A model of the value that we can add to each phase of a customer's life cycle is our trump card as a seller. We must lead with it as our entry strategy. Sometimes on a 3 × 5 card, sometimes on a computer printout, the model speaks for us. It says to the customer, Your life-cycle phase is my arena. I know how to play the game. I can help you. Here is an indication of the amount of help I can provide. Now ask me *how* I can provide this kind of help to you.

This is the model's implicit sales pitch. We do not have to say a single word about our experience or expertise. The model says it for us. Nor do we have to ask the customer to buy our product or accept our price. We have no objections to overcome, no trial closes to make over and over again, and no ethically borderline negotiation strategies to role play. When we let the model speak for us, we need only to be asked, How?

Sellers who sell from models are selling the added dollar values of their solutions. See how much value we can take away from this cost? See how much value we can add to these sales? If you want values like these, ask me *how* you can get them.

Models open the entry door for us. They get us in. They provide us with access to high-level decision-makers who manage the customer operations that are being burdened with unnecessary costs or deprived of necessary sales. They need our added values. They become our ready constituency, speaking the common language of customer operations, their problems and opportunities.

All the while, our product must remain in its carrying case or, better yet, locked in the car trunk outside or left back at the office or factory. To stand it before the customer will be fatal. It will confront the customer with a different model, not of his operations and their values but of the output from our own operations and its price. The customer will not ask, How? of these models. He will instead ask, How much? No matter what we reply, the answer will be, Too much. Our constituency will revert to, and remain with, lower-level decision-makers in the purchasing function for whom the question, How much? is their province.

3
Positioning the Solution

Specializing in Life-Cycle Solutions

The customer life-cycle phases in which we profess expertise as profit-improvers have a predictive effect on our market position. This is because positioning is self-selecting. We get the customers we are positioned for. They become our natural partners. They are attracted to us because their life-cycle phase focuses their attention on costs and we are positioned as cost reducers. Or their life-cycle phase forces their attention onto sales and we are positioned as sales developers.

If we are positioned as a *cost reducer,* we will attract two kinds of customers:

1. Startup businesses that want to avoid unnecessary sunk costs.
2. Mature businesses that want to eliminate cost centers or cut back on their downscaling impact on profits.

If we are positioned as a *sales developer,* we will attract three kinds of customers:

1. Entry businesses that want to make it fast to break-even.
2. Growth businesses that want to keep growing fast.
3. Mature businesses that want to regrow.

If we can improve customer profits by both cost reduction and sales development, we can be a full partner. Otherwise, we can only be a half partner. Whichever half we choose presents a paradox. It is easier to prove profit improvement by cost reduction because direct costs are hard numbers. Sales opportunities, on the other hand, represent opportunity losses. Their numbers are softer, more subject to assumption. But no customer can save his way to prosperity. Sooner or later, he must increase earnings from sales if he is going to grow. So sales development, which is more difficult than cost reduction to quantify as well as to achieve, is more necessary if we are going to play a commanding role in customer profit improvement.

If we can develop significant new sales for our customers, they can tolerate unnecessary costs. But if we can only reduce costs, they cannot long tolerate the lack of new sales without falling into the most stagnant mode of business—stability.

A stable business is going nowhere, neither growing nor declining. It is indecisive, inactive, and indolent. Decisions take forever. While they are being deliberated, there is hope that the need for them will go away. The stable business lives in fear. It is afraid to attempt to grow because if it tries and fails, the added investment without return will plunge it into decline. Its managers constantly look down, not up, awaiting the fall and suspecting that every action—indeed, any action—will unbalance their tentative harmony of earnings and expenses.

Stable businesses make the worst partners. They are candidates for cost reduction, but only if the costs to be reduced significantly exceed the costs incurred to reduce them and if results show up quickly. To help make sure that this is always the case, stable business managers invest as little as possible against the chance, however slight, that the funds may prove unrecoverable. Even if their investments are productive, their returns on this basis are likely to be small. The net improvement, as a result, is apt to be miniscule.

A stable business is a paradox to its own management and to any supplier business that would attempt to grow it. Businesses in stability may be grown, but they do not dare to grow. They have lost their dynamic. Only when they start to decline can they be partnerable. In the decline phase of maturity they have no choice. Sales must be developed. But, more important, costs must be reduced in a major way. The fear of falling, which induced paralysis during stability, is gone. The fear of going belly-up, which induces action, will replace it. Partners now need apply.

Positioning as the Specialist

Penetration will almost always be awarded to the specialist, rather than the generalist, supplier of products, services, systems, or solutions. The specialist knows the customer's industry. He knows the customer's business. He knows the customer's process, whose profit contribution must be improved by his solution. And he knows the customer's dependence on the process at the specific stage of his life cycle that the specialist affects. In short, the specialist knows what the customer's business objectives are at various points in the cycle and how they can be met more fully, more quickly, and more surely by making an impact on the contribution of the process.

Specializing in Startup

Startup is the single most crucial phase of the customer life cycle. Entry and growth, the two following phases, are preconditioned by startup. A good start will not necessarily predict good growth, but a poor start will largely invalidate it.

Two events take place at startup that forecast the coming attractiveness of a business. One, a market database is laid down. Two, the product's value-to-price relationship is determined. These events set the *who,* the *what,* and the *how much* for the business. If we partner at the startup phase, getting in on the ground floor, we can help influence each of these critical factors. Not only can we become invaluable, we can build ourselves into the continuing evolution of the customer's business as one of its vital components while it moves through the successive stages of its commercial life.

Specializing in Entry

For a business, entry is the "make or break" event that furnishes the proof of startup. The test of startup is how little needs to be done—or redone—at entry to refine and redefine the initial actions of the business. A good startup leaves little to be done at entry except to power up for volume operations. Rescaling output places tremendous pressure on an entry business. It threatens quality control and all the functions that are dedicated to manufacturing and marketing. Schedules must be met, downtime and recall avoided, and early warnings heeded.

Entry allows the first checkpoint at which market segmentation can be evaluated. Was the right market selected? Entry also confirms the value-to-price ratio. Will the market pay for the value? The growth phase yet to come depends on the accuracy of these startup decisions. If they are shown to be wrong at entry, growth will be delayed or denied. The business may have to go back to the drawing board—that is, back to startup—for rework.

Helping a startup business make its entry on time and on plan, and then make it through entry as quickly as possible to begin growth, is the greatest contribution we can make to a customer. Only by reaching breakeven does a business become a true commercial entity. Until then it is merely an investment, an act of faith that there is an opportunity for a profitable return. The advent of positive cash flow is the signal that faith has paid off. At this point, no one knows how much the payoff will be. But at least there will be one, and until this point is reached there can be no chance at all to make a big winner happen.

Specializing in Growth

The reward for withstanding the enormous pressure of passing quickly through entry is the privilege of accepting the prolonged pressure of growth. The growth phase of a business is its finest hour. Everything that has been planned can now come together in the race for volume—for production, for productivity, and for market share. Time is of the essence. Demand, once provoked, must be fulfilled. Competition, once enticed, must be preempted.

Two other events mark growth. The product quality, set in entry, must be standardized so that reliability becomes the product's middle name. Reliability—no surprises—is the keystone of growth. Its assurance must be warranted. At the same time that the product is being standardized for volume output, the demand that has been created for it in the marketplace must be fully met. Every unmet unit of demand represents opportunity loss. To make certain that demand is fully capitalized, growth is the phase to begin product proliferation. What is the next product going to be? How will it complement, supplement, or implement the product being grown?

If we position ourselves to partner with growth businesses, we must address three areas of customer need. We must help maximize volume. We must help enforce standardization. And we must help generate the followon products that will add up to a growth family. In these three ways, we can drive the customer's original growth curve as high as possible and hold it there as long as possible. This is in our common interest. While positive cash flow is high, new investments can be made in a successor growth curve that, at first, will reinforce its predecessor and later may replace its contribution.

Specializing in Maturity

A customer in maturity has an upside and a downside. The upside is that by the time a business has become mature, its managers know just about everything about how it should be run. However, this is also the downside. When the customer knows everything, it is difficult for him to innovate. And lack of innovation is precisely why a business becomes mature in the first place.

At maturity, the volume dependency that had been built up in growth has become chronic. The learning curve that brings unit costs down with volume is, at the same time, a stern taskmaster. As volume becomes relentless, the pressure mounts to increase the share of market necessary to absorb it. This can usually be accomplished only by accepting progressively lower margins. As a result, the watch on costs becomes a customer's main preoccupation.

If we position ourselves to partner with mature customers, we have two immediate areas of opportunity. Our transcendent duty is to keep a mature customer mature—that is, to keep him in business as a profitable entity whose return meets his corporate hurdle rate for sustained investment. Our next duty is to keep a mature customer in business *in the United States*. Otherwise, we may find that we have grown the customer but lost the business.

The art of keeping a mature customer profitable requires a fine balance between reducing costs and cost-effectively increasing sales. Cost reductions will keep a customer in the ballgame, making up for commodity-margin shrinkage. But only by adding to market share can a customer grow. Share must be sold, not bought, if it is to be a genuine contributor to renewed earnings. Since mature market size is stable at best, or more likely to be on the way down, each slice of incremental market share must come out of a competitor's share. This makes share-building expensive and frequently only transient, up for grabs by the competitor who is most willing to risk his cost control to seize it even temporarily.

Mature customers are collectors of cost centers. Even

though they acquire considerable skills in controlling costs, if we can reduce them even further we will always have a job. Since the cumulative costs at maturity are usually large, even a small percentage reduction will be welcome.

The same is true for share of market. The larger the share, the greater the value of only a small increment. In markets where the dollar value of each share point is worth several million, gains of small fractions of a single percentage point can make a considerable impact on profits. The key, of course, is that these gains must not cost more than they are worth.

With a mature customer we must ask two questions. The first is, How can we grow you? The answers will be in terms of reduced costs and increased sales. The second, which poses a greater challenge, is, How can we grow a renewed life cycle for you under the managers of your existing business?

The first question will steer us toward decreasing operating expenses, stimulating technology, and invigorating a customer's marketing functions. The second question makes an entirely different set of demands. It invites us to partner with the customer to regrow the business and make it recompetitive.

What technological opportunities can be exploited? What market opportunities? What forms of strategic alliances can be most cost-efficient: joint venture, R&D partnership, or marketing partnership? With a successful outcome, not only can we create growth, we can create a new growable customer with whom we are partnered from the inception.

Achieving Market Dominance in Our Specialty

What is the test for market dominance? Some say that it is being the market share leader, "owning" as much of the market as possible. Others say that it is being the profit leader. They base dominance on how much they take to the bank. Some businesses are fortunate. They pass both tests, being volume leader and earnings leader at the same time.

No matter which test we use, the question of dominance always has the same resolution. *We are dominant if the value we add to customer businesses is accepted as the industry standard.* Anyone who adds less automatically follows the leader.

Although it may seem that suppliers dominate markets, it is really their values that are the dominant forces. It may also seem that a supplier owns a market. But in actuality it is markets that have accepted ownership of a supplier's value. They have made it their own, setting it up as their optimal standard of performance for the business function that the supplier serves. "This cost should not exceed $100 an hour," customers say about one of their operations. How do they know? This is the norm set by the dominant supplier. "This cost center can be converted to a profit center within six to nine months." This is another dominant supplier's standard. If we can lower the standard by one month, we may be able to become dominant ourselves. If so, it will not be because of the difference of thirty days. It will be because of the dollar value of those thirty days to customer profits. Our added value will form the new standard.

As the market leader we can brand our market with the value we can contribute. The premium value of our brand gives us the privilege of putting a premium price on it. The market "buys in" to the value by paying the premium price, enabling it to achieve the standard contribution to its profits.

It is not the comparison of price to operating performance that yields a dominant value. Price-performance yields only a productivity value: units of output per units of dollars. Value is the result of comparing a profit return with the cost that must be invested to achieve it. This is done by comparative cost-benefit analysis, relating the current yield of each invested dollar to a proposed improved yield. Cost-benefit analysis produces a financial value, not an operating value. It measures dollars of return per invested dollars. It is expressed not in terms of ergs, or pounds per square inch, or bytes, but as net profit dollars and the percentage of return they represent.

Dominant standards of value are always money standards. Operating standards contribute to them, to be sure. But confronted only by performance characteristics, customers ask, What does it all add up to? How many dollars are contained in "faster"? If "faster" is truly a benefit, it will give off measurable dollars. If the dollars are truly significant, they can become the standard.

Becoming the Industry Standard

To achieve the position of life-cycle specialist, to connect the mission of our business to the mission of its core customers, is to capture the supreme differentiation—that of the *industry standard*. The standard supplier's impact on customers becomes the standard impact. No one who falls below it, or who cannot prove that he does not, can compete against the standard. Nor can anyone who may exceed the standard but cannot prove that he does. The ground rules of competition are clear. Competitors who can make an equal impact come in second. Competitors who can make only a marginally improved impact also come in second. Competitors who can make a significantly greater impact will have to prove it. They may never get the chance. What customer will abandon the industry standard on a chance? The opportunity cost would be unaffordable.

If we can position ourselves on the high ground of the industry standard, we will have two unassailable advantages. One is that we do something no one else does. The impact we make sets the standard. The other is that we know something no one else knows. The knowledge we have of customer businesses and how to bring them up to standard is exclusively our own.

As the specialist, we will have expertise composed of units of knowledge about customer operations. Our impact will be composed of units of profits added to customer bottom lines. In this way, our position as the industry standard can be self-perpetuating. Specifications may say "IBM or equal," but they specify IBM as the yardstick. Performance must be

"IBM-compatible," but it is with IBM performance that compatibility must be achieved. IBM is the industry standard. Everyone else is "other." The equals come in second.

As the specialist, we will be the standard of knowledge about the customer business functions we affect. Customers will turn first to us for information. We can tell them the one thing they need most to know: how they compare with industry norms. The norms belong to the specialist. It is we who know how cost-free, how productive, and how revenue-producing the customer's functions *can be*. In other words, we know how far each customer departs from the standard. If a customer is below the standard, we can hire on to bring him closer to the norm. If a customer is already above the standard, we can work to keep him there or, better yet, to *improve* his superiority over the norm. This is how we will penetrate.

The Specialist Mission

Our mission as the specialist is clear. No one has to ask twice what we do. We possess our customer industry's norms. We keep our customers on or below the norms in the area of costs. We keep customers on or above norms in the areas of productivity and sales revenues. We are, in effect, a health maintenance organization for business. Below par? Regain your health; practice remedial medicine. At or above par? Maintain your health; practice preventive medicine.

Our mission as the specialist is to improve the profit contribution of the customer operations that we affect. This gives our customers three opportunities to disadvantage their competitors. They can be a lower-cost supplier. They can be a more productive supplier. Or they can be the most profitable seller because of higher quality, lower cost, or better ability to lower the cost, improve the productivity, or increase the sales of their customers.

The ultimate advantage that we can confer on our customers is *to help them become the industry standard in their own markets*.

Ruling Out Debate

Competition debilitates margins. Among startup businesses, competition can delay entry and foreshorten their growth phase by neutralizing merits and forcing commodity status even on new products. Among mature businesses, competition clones all attempts at differentiation and thereby stifles price at low levels of profit. It also adds to sales cost, further weakening already depleted margins.

Only the industry standard-bearer is immune to debate on the comparative merits of his product, system, or service. The question he is asked by customers concerns *how:* How can I achieve or exceed the industry standard? The one he avoids from customers is the *how-much* question: How much is your product?

The answer to the *how* question is a proposal. The answer to the *how-much* question is a reduced price. To the customer who asks how much, almost any price will be too much.

There are only two ways that a price suspected of being too much can be justified. One is to give away with it some free goods or services, thereby sweetening the deal. The other is to plead on the basis of superior performance merits. If a pleader cannot be best, he must try to be better. Today and forever more, hardly anyone can be best for long. Even being better—enough better to make price commensurate with value—is increasingly difficult to achieve and less likely to be maintained on an exclusive basis.

Debates on the merits of competitive products inevitably become debates on comparative price. The specialist who establishes the industry standard rules out debate on the merits of his products or the relationship between their value and his price. He sells a different product than his competitors: the added value of an improved profit contribution.

By shielding his products from debate on their merits, the industry standard-bearer protects them from margin erosion. He also defends them against the need for ever-enlarging investments to realize the elusive and transitory objective of performance superiority. Competitors find it difficult to get at him. They try to encourage debate on the merits. Yet he, meanwhile, is resolving a very different kind of debate that he has stimulated, and will referee, within his customer organizations: How can we improve the profit contribution of your operations? Product merits generally play a small role in this debate. No wonder, as competitors complain, the customer is not listening.

Positioning As the Mixmaster

Each life-cycle stage is a mix of costs and opportunities. Where the customer's mix is concerned, can we help it more nearly deliver its optimal contribution to profit? If we can learn how to master the mix of customer costs in an industry's manufacturing process, for example, we can protect our role as the industry's standard-bearer.

Every customer allocates certain resources to each of his functions. This is his asset base—or, more accurately, his cost base. Some of these resources are supplied internally: his own people and the capital they use. The rest of his resources come from outside—the products, services, and systems purchased from a variety of suppliers. Taken together, these internal and external resources are the customer's current operating "mix." In order to penetrate, we will have to help create a mix that will contribute higher profits or greater opportunity.

All customer businesses operate with a mix. Some mixes are simply conglomerations of products. Others include services such as training or maintenance. Others are composed of systems, which, in turn, are composed of subsystems. We must determine where we fit in the mix, what we can contribute to it, and what improvements we can propose.

The mix becomes our "market." It is where we fit, where we operate, where we belong. It will become the arena of our expertise. We must know how to make it produce profits in the most cost-effective manner, and we must know this better than anyone else. We must master the mix so well that we can position ourselves with customers as their industry's "mixmaster."

Customer mixes usually lag behind the optimal mix. They frequently represent a sizable investment. They also are tied to a customer's learning curve. His people have learned how to operate the current mix and, over time, they have become familiar with its capabilities and its quirks. Training programs have been built around it. Cost and production schedules are established for it. Psychologically, it has become "the way we do things around here"—the "corporate culture." It must be approached remedially but respectfully. We do not want to run our customers' businesses. We want to partner with them so that *they can run them better.*

There are three strategies for helping a customer achieve an optimal operating mix.

1. We can supplant one or more elements in his current mix. If the mix is labor intensive, for example, we may be able to reduce labor content by substituting an automated process or eliminating an operation altogether. Or we may be able to combine separate processes, such as forecasting and inventory control, thereby eliminating overlapping and duplicated costs.

2. We can substitute our product or process for a competitive product or process that is part of the customer's current mix. The basis for our recommendation must be that improved financial benefits will accrue to the customer if the mix is altered, not simply that more advantageous performance benefits will be realized.

3. We can restructure the mix in such a significant manner that we will be the most knowledgeable expert about its operation and its contribution to improved profits. In addition to realizing improved profits by becoming our partner, customers may consider the prestige of working with us, the industry innovator, an extra motivation.

Tables 3-1 and 3-2 show a format for auditing a customer's mix (in this case a mix of medical instruments) in terms of its configuration and financial impact. In Table 3-1, the configuration is shown before the optimal mix is achieved. Table 3-2 shows the optimal mix format. Figure 3-1 is the financial-analysis format for determining the dollar value of the optimal mix.

The specific tactics of penetrating by means of helping the customer achieve an optimal mix will depend on the industry we serve. If we sell personal care products to major supermarket and drug chains, we can penetrate by making optimal use of the number of facings that stores allocate to our products versus those of competitors, the location of our fac-

Table 3-1. **Present equipment-configuration analysis.**

	# Year	$ Price	Annual $ Cost
Equipment			
Instrument A	————	————	————
Instrument B	————	————	————
Instrument C	————	————	————
Instrument D	————	————	————
Accessory Sets			
Set 1	————	————	————
Set 2	————	————	————
Set 3	————	————	————
Set 4	————	————	————
Materials			
Material XX	————	————	————
Material YY	————	————	————
Material ZZ	————	————	————

ings, and the types of displays. The proof of our success will have to be quantified in financial benefits, such as profit improvement per square foot, overall improvement from the personal care department's profit contribution per store, or improved profit contribution from related-item sales.

If we sell financial services like stocks and bonds, insurance, real estate investments, or money market funds to affluent individuals, we can achieve an optimal mix of their portfolios in terms of growth potential, risk, and current payout. The proof of our success will have to be quantified in dollar benefits, such as higher earnings, lower taxes, or increased net worth.

The Specialist Mystique

Companies composed of many more or less related businesses must disconnect them from each other and from their agglom-

Table 3-2. *Optimal equipment-configuration analysis.*

	# Year	$ Price	Annual $ Cost
Equipment			
Instrument A-B	————	————	————
Instrument C	————	————	————
Accessory Sets			
Set 1-2	————	————	————
Set 3	————	————	————
Materials			
Material XX	————	————	————
Material YY	————	————	————

erated mass before they can act as specialists in a customer life cycle. They must focus on each of their principal businesses as if it were their *only* business—which, of course, it is to customers. This process requires reorganization, often accompanied by divestiture.

Lockheed became a defense business specialist because it wrote off commercial aircraft. Texas Instruments became a specialist in applied computer technology because it divested its home computer business. Allied-Signal became a specialist in electronics and chemicals because it packaged dozens of commodity businesses, together with their managers, in di-

Figure 3-1. **Before and after financial analysis.**

Depreciation

> Total annual instrument depreciation $_____
> (Total number of instruments × average price per useful life)

Lease Cost

> Total annual instrument lease cost $_____
> (Total number of leased instruments × average lease cost per month × 12)

Maintenance

> Total annual instrument maintenance cost $_____
> (Total leased instruments × Total purchased instruments × Average annual maintenance cost)

Interest on Purchase Price

> $$\frac{Total\ instruments\ purchased \times Average\ purchase\ price \times Cost\ of\ money}{100}$$

---

verse fields like bearings, soda ash, and pollution control, and spun them all out into a separate corporation.

General Telephone & Electronics became a specialist in regulated telephone operations because it moved out of its one attempt to penetrate high-technology telecommunications in the unregulated market. It goes on managing in the way it has become comfortable, making decisions by consensus, setting up task forces on how to make decisions faster, and issuing cards containing the company's "seven core values" so that its managers can compare operations to those of competitors— other mature, regulated utilities.

Singer became a specialist by spinning off the 135-year-old sewing machine operations that made it a household name and concentrating on aerospace electronics.

Kodak has shrunk its core photographic business so that it can specialize in joint ventures, minority investments, and acquisitions in electronic publishing, antiviral and antiaging biotechnologies, and software information systems. To get to the point where it could take a specialist point of view, Kodak had to cut its silver-based film work force by almost 25,000 employees in two years. Decisions about making the transition to specialization had gone up and down chains of command for years, each taking several months and being biased by the feeling that Kodak "didn't need to take risks" or shouldn't make decisions without ceaseless testing and retesting first.

When its revision was completed and Kodak had organized to specialize in the four businesses of photography, information services, chemicals, and life sciences, management acknowledged its difficulties this way: "We intellectually wanted to form the groups two years ago, but we had this long history of the company centering on the photographic."

By bringing focus to their businesses, multibusiness companies like Kodak can practice the premier principle of penetration strategy: concentration. In this way, they can achieve the expert position, the essential ingredient of penetration strategy. It is not expertise in their own product or its processing that will make them stand out. Rather, it is expertise in their customers' operations so that they can improve the contributions they make to customer profits.

Large, multibusiness companies can become multiple specialists. The central question to ask before getting into a business should be, Can we be the leading specialist? If not, why get in?

The Xomox Model

Xomox Corporation is an exemplary model of specialist strategy. It manufactures sleeve valves, which have essentially the same basic form and concept as the lead valves that were found in the ruins of Pompeii in 79 A.D. It is therefore an understatement to say that the valve business is mature. Not only that, it is oversupplied by 300 manufacturers. Yet Xomox, a small company, has consistently earned 30 percent average return on equity, the reward of the specialist.

The Xomox strategy is threefold: concentrate, customize, and consult.

Xomox *concentrates* on a single product that it sells principally to a single industry, petrochemicals.

Xomox *customizes* its valves to fit specific chemical processes.

Xomox sells valves but it *consults* on their applications engineering and bases its prices on the value added to each process by decreasing its costs or improving its productivity. It is paid a premium price for the value it adds, not the valves it sells. The value is an amalgam of valves, applications engineering, service, and customer training. But the core value is Xomox's knowledge of petrochemicals processing. It knows where the costs cluster at startup, in growth, and at maturity; by how much it can reduce them; and what the dollar value of those reduced costs can amount to. It also knows where productivity can be improved, by how much it can improve output, and what the dollar value of that improved output—and its effect on sales—can be at each stage of the customer life cycle.

As *the* specialist in petrochemicals processing, Xomox knows more about how to apply valve technology to reduce costs and increase productivity than its customers can know or that its competitors have learned. That is one aspect of its specialist positioning. The other is that Xomox knows more about how to translate its applications into new customer profits than either its customers or its competitors.

To say that Xomox enjoys its premier position because it is an *applier* of valves instead of merely a *supplier* of them is to short-cut the point. The question is, what does Xomox specialize in applying? The answer is not valves but the application of improved profits to petrochemical processes. That is the Xomox specialty.

The reason this specialty makes money for Xomox is that it is also the specialty of Xomox customers. This is the essence of the power of specialization that no generalist can match. As the specialist supplier, Xomox has found the penetration connection: the way to connect its mission to the mission of the market.

What is the Xomox secret? Xomox knows something that its competitors do not: crucial *data* about improving the operations of its customer processes. Xomox has equipped itself with this capability as the basis for its competitive positioning. Its position is based on data—business function information that helps Xomox reduce customer costs and market information that helps Xomox increase customer sales.

The Specialist's Knowledge Base

In his files and in his head, the specialist carries around a database that immediately positions him as an expert. If he is a functional specialist, his database will be filled with the norms of the customer business functions that he can improve. If he is a sales developer—a market specialist—his database will contain sales norms and strategies for bringing the customer's products closer to them.

Business Function Database

If we are going to improve a customer's profit by reducing his costs, we must work from a base of knowledge about the processes that contribute to his costs. To be "process-smart" about the operations of his business, we must know four types of growth facts:

1. We must know what our competition is. This means knowing the current costs that are being thrown off by the customer's operations. He competes against these costs daily. We must help him be a better competitor by learning even more about them. We can help him quantify them more exactly. We can also share with him our knowledge of his industry's average costs so he can calculate his variances and bring them into line.

2. We must have a strategy for applying our expertise against our competition. This means knowing how to reduce our customer's current costs. We must know the most cost-effective approach to each problem; its optimal mix of our products and services; and the most expeditious, least disruptive manner of implementing this approach in the customer's ongoing operations.

3. We must know the norms for reducing a function's costs by applying our solution. This means knowing how much of a dollar difference our system can make to a customer's operation before we install it, how quickly the difference will make itself felt, and how much assurance we can give the customer that he can count on receiving the difference. We must also know how frequently to monitor and measure the difference so that it can be validated.

4. We must know what is a fair investment for the customer to make in exchange for the difference between his current cost and our norm. This means knowing the value of the difference to the customer: how significant it will be to the value of his business, the added value of the speedy realization of the released funds, and how much it is worth to him to have a high degree of certainty that the new profits will flow to him

in the promised amounts over the predicted time frame. On this basis we can set a fair price for the products and services we will provide.

Customer's Customers' Databases

If we are going to improve a customer's profit by helping him to increase his sales, we must work from a base of knowledge about his markets. To be "market-smart," we must know four types of growth facts:

1. We must first know what our competition is. This means knowing the current profits being contributed by our customer's customers. He competes to increase those profits daily. We must help him be a better competitor by learning even more about his customers. We can help him quantify his profits from them more exactly. We can also share our knowledge of his customers' industries so that he can identify his own best growth partners and assign a priority order to partnering with them.

2. We must have a strategy for applying our expertise against our competition. This means knowing how to increase the customer's current profitable sales from his existing customer base and how to extend that base to include new customers.

3. We must know the most cost-effective approach for each customer market; its optimal mix of our products and services; and the most electrifying, least vulnerable manner of capturing the market.

4. We must know the norms for increasing a product's sales by applying our kind of solution. This means knowing how much of a dollar difference our system can make to a customer's product performance before we install it, how quickly the difference will make itself felt, and how much assurance we can give the customer that he can count on receiving the difference from our solution. We must also know how frequently to monitor and measure the dollar difference so that it can be validated.

The Classic Penetration Database

The APACHE® model is the classic penetration database. APACHE is the acronym for Accelerated Penetration At Customer High Levels of Earnings.* It contains an inventory of the major cost problems whose solutions we can apply to a key customer. It also contains an inventory of each customer's major unrealized sales opportunities with his customers, which represent his own partnership opportunities. Matched with them will be our solutions: the products and services that compose them, their costs, and their most likely contributions to profit. If our solutions can diminish our customer's costs, we can elevate his rate of return. If we can also enhance his profitable sales volume, we can further elevate his return rate.

In our joint APACHE databases, we come together in a knowledge alliance with our growth partners. Their problems and opportunities mix and match with our solutions. How can an APACHE be begun?

Getting to know an industry and its customers is a two-stage effort. It is a front-end-loaded undertaking, but, once structured, the database is simple and inexpensive to keep up to date. The first stage is to learn as much as we can from the multiple sources that are always available without going to our customers themselves. Then when we take on the second and third stages that deal specifically with our customers, we will have two advantages: (1) we will already know something about their businesses, so we will have less to ask of customers; and (2) we will have a meaningful framework on which to hang the information they share with us.

In addition to the ubiquitous publications and knowledgeable professionals of the U.S. government, especially the Departments of State and Commerce, six additional sources can provide information about the costs and revenue potential of our domestic and global customers.

1. The first and most obvious source is our own people.

* APACHE® is the registered trademark of Mack Hanan's program for key-account databases and penetration proposals.

Some of them may have been recruited from customer industries, and some may even have worked for key customers. Others may have participated in market research studies that produced information relevant to our partnering needs. If we maintain a library, its periodicals and publications—especially the trade magazines of our key industries—can be culled for data. A good public library can be a valuable adjunct in obtaining published information of all types.

2. Trade associations in our customers' industries are staffed by people who usually devote their careers to their trade. They have access to both general and specific information about individual companies. Associations also maintain libraries of industry norms and computerized market databases.

3. Securities analysts are professional researchers of specific industries employed by brokerage houses to follow these industries over long periods of time. They publish updated industry analyses evaluating customer growth potential, highlighting the major factors that determine profits and costs, and defining trends that can forecast opportunities. Many analysts will provide personal counsel when information can be exchanged on a *quid pro quo* basis.

4. Industry experts and consultants can be retained on a one-time or periodic basis to lay a foundation for understanding an industry's operations and cost structure. Experts can be helpful in estimating the impact of our technology versus competitive technologies on customer costs and productivity. In addition, they can give us information about business-function problems afflicting an industry and about the problems of individual companies and the strategies they are currently implementing, or plan to implement, to solve them.

5. Other suppliers who sell noncompetitive products and services to our key customers may have acquired knowledge of customer costs and sales opportunities they will share with us. Their information will probably reflect their own interests, however, which may make their data peripheral to our needs. Nonetheless, we may be able to translate what they know into the way our own business cuts into customer costs.

6. Companies in the same industry that are not key accounts are sometimes easier to approach for general information than our own major customers. They operate the same business functions, and their costs tend to cluster at the same critical choke points. The potential sales opportunities of the industry affect them in the same way they affect our key accounts. Even though their businesses are different in many respects from those of our prime customers, they offer enough clues to make their cultivation worthwhile.

Putting a Penetration Database to Work

Dresser-Wayne offers an unparalleled example, worthy of widespread emulation, of making a penetration database work. The company is a mature manufacturer and marketer of retail management control systems. It supplies single-source systems to major oil company retail outlets and service stations, independent service stations, and convenience stores that sell gasoline. Its systems consist of gas dispenser pumps, electronic control consoles that operate and monitor the pumps, automatic cash registers, automatic service equipment, and data storage and handling capabilities.

To the individual gas station retailer, the foremost benefits of Dresser-Wayne's systems are timely profit reports on sales. They provide the flexibility to change pricing quickly to correspond to peak and off-peak driving hours, as well as accurate cost control and inventory data. The systems safeguard against downtime. They can also lower the costs of station design by calculating space savings and increases in the throughput of customer traffic within the smaller space.

The retailer's home office also benefits by receiving data on sales and inventory faster and more accurately, which in turn can allow improvements in the delivery schedules to each station. In addition, one supervisor at the head office can manage twelve stations instead of six, saving high-priced labor costs at the supervisor level.

Dresser-Wayne is equipped with an APACHE database. Each market segment—the major oil companies, the independents, and the convenience stores—has its individual database, but the general benefits that Dresser-Wayne can offer to all three of its markets are similar: improved profits through increased sales, and reduced costs with greater security and control. The specific benefits vary with the market segment and the problem to be solved and, accordingly, Dresser-Wayne's APACHE is organized to provide answers to questions like these:

1. Where is the problem at the station level? Is it principally an inventory-control problem based on poor cash management? Is it a credit-control problem? Are receipts and distribution at the heart of the problem? Or is it a question of labor skills, quality of maintenance, or inefficiency of present station design and a resulting loss of customer throughput?
2. Where is the problem at the home-office level? Is it a problem of data control and reporting, cash management, or supervisory management?
3. Is this a product sales opportunity or a system selling opportunity? Is there opportunity here for the sale of a supersystem composed of several gas pumps, monitoring consoles, a cash-management control system, data-storage and data-handling modems, and a training program?
4. Is this a lease or a buy opportunity?
5. Is there an opportunity to sell a plan to reconstruct individual gas stations to increase traffic, or is it more cost-effective to focus on improving station profit contribution from existing layouts?
6. What are the total costs to be reduced? What are the total sales revenues to be gained? What are the investment offsets required to achieve these results? What net profit will result? What is the return on investment?

APACHE reports on the total number of outlets that can be affected in each chain and identifies each outlet as either among the top 10 percent, in the middle, or among "all others," specifying the average number of gallons each outlet moves each month along with other products and services. Data are also included on each station manager's purchase habits, work force and its cost structure, and use of competitive equipment. Similar information is also available on home-office managers.

Dresser-Wayne's APACHE information is shown in Figures 3-2 through 3-4. These three figures, representing computer display screens, are devoted to the convenience-store segment of the market.

On the Problem/Opportunity Summary Screen in Figure 3-2, APACHE shows the monthly profit currently contrib-

Figure 3-2. **Problem/opportunity summary screen.**

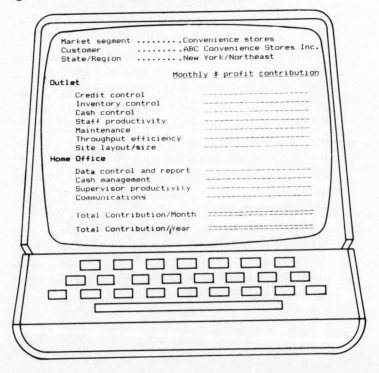

uted by key outlets in the ABC Convenience Stores chain lo-
cated in New York State. Some of these dollar values are positive, but others are negative. The positive values may indicate
sales opportunities for Dresser-Wayne if they are lower than
average; the negative values may indicate sales opportunities
if they can be reduced or eliminated.

APACHE also reveals the contributions to profit being
made by the chain's home office. These may provide supplementary sales opportunities.

If the inventory control function shows a negative profit
contribution or only a small positive contribution to the
chain's profit, it can then be analyzed up close as a separate
problem area on the screen shown on Figure 3-3. The problem of stock-out can be intensively evaluated according to its
gallonage and dollar values. If Dresser-Wayne believes it can

Figure 3-3.   **Problem analysis screen.**

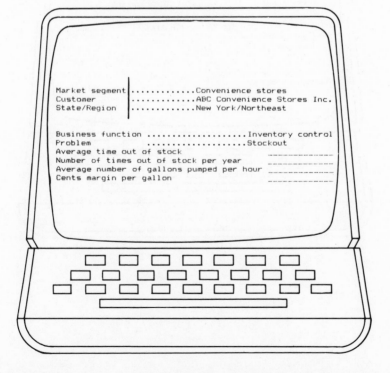

improve this area, it may create a proposal that will compare customer improvement with the current situation. APACHE will then show Figure 3-4, pointing out the dollar benefits that Dresser-Wayne can bring to the customer on a weekly and monthly basis for any individual store or for the entire ABC chain. On this foundation, penetration can begin.

Figure 3-4.   **Benefit-analysis screen.**

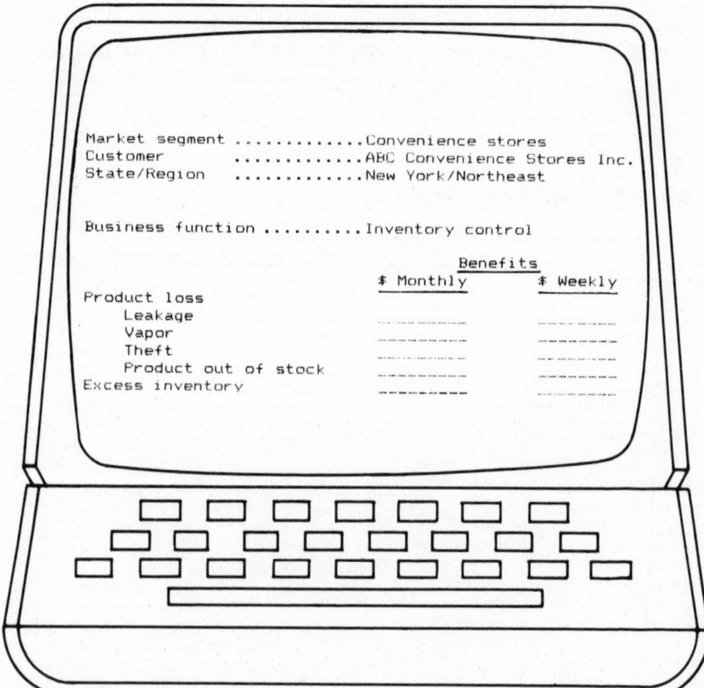

4
Organizing the Teams

Structuring Cycle-Compatible Growth Teams

Penetrating by partnering is a team task. It requires a leader who manages a group of partners in customer profit improvement. The partners, in turn, require a similar team of customer partners as their correlates. When the two teams themselves become partners, penetration occurs.

A penetration team's managing partner plays the role that enhances the traditional province of a sales representative. The manager must be more than a representative of the supplier to the customer; he must be a customer's partner, whose added values, both personal and team, make him a necessary player if the customer's problems are to be solved and his opportunities capitalized in the most cost-effective way.

Penetration teams are sales teams, but they must do much more than make sales. They must improve customer profits. This is the basis on which they sell, positioning themselves as the delivery mechanism for new customer profits. They must be ready, willing, and able to implement, to apply their resources to the customer's business. For this reason, they must be led by a manager who directs what is, in effect, a small business unit of key resources who are organized along entrepreneurial lines and who can fit into a partnerable relationship with the customer.

The Managing Partner

A partner-in-charge heads up the penetration team. He or she will be the correlate of the customer's partner-in-charge. The partners-in-charge will manage their penetration teams, be responsible for resourcing them properly, and employ them in partnership with each other so that the proposed profits from penetration can be achieved.

The managing partner can be likened to an orchestra leader who also plays an instrument. He is charged with setting the penetration plan's objectives and the most cost-effective strategy for achieving them. As the leader, the manager is surrounded by a small group of supportive players, who contribute their specialities when needed. If the supplier's business is small or just making its entrepreneurial entry, the leader and the small group of players may be the entire corporate orchestra. As the supplier's business matures, however, its bench strength increases and many other specialists become available for call when the notes they can hit need to be played.

A supplier team's leader manages the partnering of his own and the customer's team. Fairly or not, the customer will evaluate the caliber of the supplier's resources—and business—through the team manager. The customer will ask, Are these our kind of people? Do they share our objectives? Can they implement? Will they work smoothly with our people and gain their acceptance as full working partners, or will they prove disruptive and unproductive? When all is said and done, will they have brought to the party anything that we could not have done for ourselves? Or done better in a partnership with someone else?

If the answers to these questions are to be affirmative, the supplier's managing partner will be largely responsible. The manager's self-conduct, and the way the team is staffed, structured, and deployed, will be the main determinants.

Remarkable Qualities

These expectations clearly require the manager to be a remarkable person—remarkable in the literal sense of being worthy of remark. A remarkable manager, who is, after all, a supplier's key account penetrator, must know four things:

1. *The customer's business*—its main cost problems at its current stage of the life cycle and its main opportunities to increase revenues.
2. *The customer's values*—the dollar value of each of the customer's current costs and each lost sales opportunity.
3. *The supplier's replacement values*—the dollar value of each of the customer's costs and opportunities *after* the supplier's solutions are installed.
4. *The supplier's business*—the most cost-effective way the supplier's values can be installed and the minimal resource team that can make and monitor the installation.

This base of knowledge, required to penetrate as a partner, should be supplemented by four personal characteristics:

1. *Empathy*—the ability to commit to the customer's profit objectives as if they were the manager's own.
2. *Drive*—the power to direct the supplier's resources against the customer's objectives in a true alliance of equals.
3. *Sharing*—the need to reveal, and have the customer team reveal, information vital to the partnership's success in a consistently open manner.
4. *A Kingmaker Approach*—the contentment of realizing personal ambitions and rewards by making the *customer manager* a king.

Compensation Plans

How should such a remarkable person as a managing partner be rewarded? There are three main types of incentive compensation plans for managing partners and their teams.

Plan One: Compensation for Up-Front Development and Release from Quota

This is the most basic compensation plan. It acknowledges the need for the managing partner and team members to invest more up-front development time to prepare penetration than vending traditionally requires. This distortion of the sales cycle places an unaccustomed burden on its front end, although it does not normally prolong the cycle's total duration. Plan One attempts to compensate for this expenditure of customer-development time by either a fixed cash award or a retroactive reward based on the eventual size of the customer's order when penetration has been achieved. When compensation for development is based on its eventual result, it resembles pay for performance rather than simply for time.

Compensation to develop penetration makes a team's preparatory work affordable to its members. Unless the managing partners are released from their vendor quotas, however, there will be neither time nor incentive to prepare. Plan One is therefore double-barreled. Quota assignments for managing partners must be reduced and in some cases abandoned altogether.

Plan Two: Compensation Based on the Customer's Investment

To encourage a commitment of penetration, Plan Two compensates managing partners and their teams for the amount of the customer's investment—in effect, the size of the order. This is the total dollar amount of the customer's expenditure for the supplier's products and services, similar to the traditional reward system for vendor sales. In some cases, the team that makes the penetration will receive followon payments for future sales that are derived from penetration.

Plan Two is easy to combine with Plan One. When this is done, both preparation for penetration and its achievement are rewarded.

Plan Three: Compensation Based on the Customer's Return

This is the most advanced compensation plan. Its purpose is to encourage the commitment of managing partners and their teams to their customers. The plan rewards them for the same result that governs the customer's reward—the size of his profits. This bases compensation not on what a customer spends but on what he earns from his expenditure, thereby bonding the team to the customer's success. Behind this plan is the assumption that the purpose of penetration is not simply to sell—that the true objective of partnering a customer to penetrate his business is to do what the customer himself wants to do: grow his business. Penetration in this manner puts all the partners from both sides in the same boat. Everybody wins or nobody does.

Plan Three removes all doubt from a customer's mind that his supplier is committed to their mutual success. It makes clear that the supplier's interest and the customer's interest are the same, giving the concept of partnership its ultimate reality.

The Lean Team

A managing partner's penetration team should be lean. Its resources should include only those that are necessary to ensure penetration. The basic penetration team will provide three resources, whose organization is shown in Figure 4-1.

1. The *Financial Resource* embodies the skills of quantifying Profit Improvement Proposals in terms of the

net present value of proposed profits and the rate of return they represent on the customer's investment.

2. The *Technical Resource* embodies the skills of applying the supplier's system to the customer's operations so that the proposed profit improvement is realized.

3. The *Data Resource* embodies the skills of collecting, accessing, and interpreting information about the improvements in customer costs, productivity, and sales and comparing them against the supplier's norms.

Led by an aggressive, sensitive manager, a lean team like this represents a microcosm of the supplier's ability to improve customer profits. It says to its customers, We know your problems and opportunities, we can improve their contributions to profits, and we can quantify our improvement.

Whenever necessary, a lean team can be supplemented by additional internal resources and by independent outside experts. If a supplier's customers are at entry or early growth in

Figure 4-1. **Lean-team organization.**

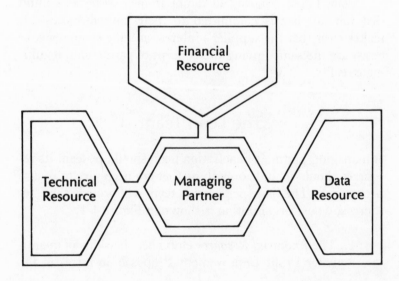

their life cycles, the basic team will almost always suffice. As customer size and complexity enlarge with protracted growth and maturity, augmentation becomes more necessary in areas such as research and engineering, manufacturing, or specialty aspects of sales such as direct marketing and telemarketing.

All teams, large or small, have the same penetration mission: to implement their skills in the customer's business.

Until they do, the true definition of the "capabilities" they represent is simply "cost." Only by applying their abilities to customer problems and opportunities can they convert costs to profits for the supplier who employs them or for their customer. Every day it is "out of work" the team incurs the costs of lost opportunity for both parties.

What is the best way to get a lean team quickly employed? Instead of asking for an order, it is by proposing that the customer organize a correlate team so that penetration, as well as the implementation to follow, can be a joint enterprise. The customer's team should contain the same categories of capability—finance, technical, and data—and should be led by its own managing partner. This will permit the two teams to partner not only at the top but also at the individual levels of each resource.

When the customer provides his team and the two teams sit down together to begin planning the joint implementation of the supplier's Profit Improvement Proposal, penetration has begun.

The Strategic Penetration Unit

A supplier's penetration teams are the delivery mechanisms for the profits he improves for his customers. They therefore require a broader statement of mission than traditional sales teams that vend goods and services. True enough, their transcendent objective is to sell. But because they sell profits, not products, they affect a customer's business far beyond his purchase functions—in the enhanced contributions they make to his net worth, his capital funds, and his cash flow and liquidity. These are business results, not just the results of purchasing policy or vendor relations. They bring penetration teams into intimate and continuing contact with a customer's most vital processes: beyond his manufacturing or marketing operations and into his moneymaking functions. A team that behaves this way is more than a sales team. It is *a business,* a microcosm of the supplier's business as a whole.

A penetration team has several characteristics that we associate with a business. It is led by a manager who has, at a minimum, revenue responsibility and, under Compensation Plan Three, can have profit responsibility as well. It has dedicated resources and a source of supply. It serves a definable market, has financial objectives, possesses a database on its market's needs, and has the ability to enter into contracts to fulfill those needs. Freed from conventional organization thinking, the penetration team can fairly be regarded as a Strategic Penetration Unit (SPU) of its company.

By recognizing the way it is organized, the way it operates, and the type of mission it is chartered to perform, we can see the Strategic Penetration Unit for what it really is: a startup business that must make its entry into the customer businesses that compose its market as quickly as possible. As a startup, the SPU is subject to the same pressures of its own life-cycle phase that customer startups face. It represents an investment from which a return is expected. It must push through to entry, generate positive cash flow, and become a growth business. And it must achieve these objectives in the same manner that its customer startups proceed to market: It must partner with a customer business by reducing costs or increasing sales revenues.

As a startup business, an SPU requires the two essential capabilities of every startup. First of all, *it must make sales.* Since it is structured as a sales team, it should be ideally suited to sell. Second, *it must make profitable sales.* The improved customer profits that it proposes must be delivered exactly as they are proposed, both in terms of how much and how soon. This means that the solution systems that it implements in a customer's business must "work" according to profit specifications as well as operating performance specifications. Otherwise, they cannot maximize their profits to the SPU.

Like all startups, successful penetration teams can look forward to moving through the progressive phases of the business life cycle. They must maintain a rising rate of growth— for their customers as well as themselves—and defend against the erosive inroads of maturity. They must resist the temptation to grow mature along with the customer, for this is the surest invitation to surprise departnering. In the famous last words of one team's managing partner: "Only last week they told me what a great guy they thought I was and how much we had helped them over the years and now—all of a sudden, like overnight—we've lost the account. How could I have stopped being such a great guy, and how could we have stopped helping them, in just seven days?"

The best defense against departnering at maturity is a tripartite strategy: disdaining complacency, continually innovating the application of the solution systems that improve customer profit, and reinvigorating the penetration team leadership and resources. How can the early inquisitiveness of the startup team be maintained? How can applications be applied more broadly and deeply across customer operations? How can profits be further improved? These drive forces are part of the founder's thrust in startup organizations. They mobilize success. When such questions are no longer being asked or answered, new penetrations may be denied and original penetrations may be sealed off from additional growth, or replaced.

Making Penetration a Business

Once a penetration team is structured as a business unit, charged with profit responsibility for itself and profit improvement for its customers, the role of the managing partner undergoes a change. He or she is no longer the sales representative of old; nor, for that matter, the national account manager. A penetration team's managing partner must be repositioned as an entrepreneurial business manager with P & L responsibility for growing the business of the Strategic Penetration Unit. Instead of a quota based on revenues, the manager will be judged on profits: "profits accrued" and "profits improved." The team's resources will be charged against his earnings, as will its other operating costs. The team's revenue-to-investment ratio will still be interesting at top management levels. Of even greater meaning, however, will be the return-on-investment ratio, which will tell how well the manager is converting the team's capabilities into capital.

Major account sales have become too important to leave to sales representatives. Key customers account for the 20 percent or less of sales that can yield up to 80 percent or more of profits. They are the core of every supplier's market. Cost-effective selling is impossible without them. Major accounts not only control today's profitable sales volume, they also represent every supplier's best prospects for future sales. Losing a major account, therefore, does more than deprive us of current profits. It saddles us with an inescapable loss of future profits, a loss that will generally be costly and time-consuming to make up—if indeed we can.

The Business Manager's Mindset

As the crucial importance of major accounts becomes better understood, selling to them has undergone successive alteration. It has moved away from selling products, services, and systems in a competitive "my product versus their product" sense into an arena composed of three requirements:

1. *Educating* the customer in how to improve the profit contribution from his operations.
2. *Consulting* with the customer on how to increase profits, accelerate their flow, and certify their attainment.
3. *Collaborating* with the customer on how to implement solution systems for maximum profit contribution, how to plan jointly for a continuous contribution, and

how to measure and monitor results from the partnership.

These requirements are not served by traditional selling
skills. Nor are they served by a supplier's product knowledge
or competitive awareness. They can be met only by a different
kind of competitiveness than we usually associate with the
sales function—competitiveness against the same objectives
our customers compete against. There are two of them. One
is a customer's competition against his costs. Can we help him
win over them by avoiding some and reducing others? The
second is a customer's competition against his own competitors. Can we help him come out ahead by increasing his sales
and share of the market?

What kind of mindset is best able to respond to these
challenges? It is the mindset of the business manager, someone who runs his or her own business and can say two things
about it: (1) *how profits are made* and how to improve them;
(2) *how profits are made in the customer's business* and how to
improve them. These are the minimum requirements for handling the job. They allow the manager to get upstairs in each
customer company to sell at high levels where only the language of business is spoken. And they allow the manager to
speak the language of each customer's own industry, thereby
permitting partnership to take place.

Industry Dedication

What is industry language composed of? Qualitative con-
versation is just the parsley around the steak; the beef itself is
an industry's numbers. These include the norms for its principal cost clusters and the dollar values that can accrue from
improving them: for example, a 1 percent increase in market
share to bring a sales process closer to the industry average of
sales productivity can be expected to yield X dollars in improved profit contribution.

This is industry-think. It is expressed in industry-speak.

From a customer's vantage point, a penetration team manager who cannot think this way is not thinking. A penetration team manager who cannot speak this way—who cannot speak as "we" but only speaks with the vendor's "I"—is not saying anything.

This means that a Strategic Penetration Unit must be dedicated to each of the two industries in which its customer businesses operate—their own industry where they manufacture and the industry where they market. There can be no substitute for industry dedication. There is no other way of knowing what to educate a customer about; or consult with him about; or collaborate with him in his own frame of reference in his own language. To be anything other than an industry specialist with major customers is to be a vendor to them: to sell on the basis of price and performance, to compete for narrowing margins against similar performing competitors at cost-plus prices, and to miss out over and over again on the big-winner sales that are being made by the specialists who penetrate at the top.

5
Proposing the Added Values

Closing the Sale by Adding Life-Cycle Values

We must meet two requirements if we are to condense our sales cycle and close penetrations quickly: We must specialize in improving profits, not selling products, and we must specialize in improving profits for a specific market. Our market must be *specified*—that is, specifications for its profitability must be our prime offering. The specifications must be based on (1) the norms of the customer's industry and (2) the life-cycle phase of each customer's business that we seek to penetrate.

When we come to call, we must bring along our "models." A model is a representation of improved profits that we have made happen in the past; it can predict the amount and rate of future profits that we can improve. In this sense, a model is the distillation of our expertise. Using it as a template, we can fit its frame over a customer's operations. Where the frame's profit borders are *better* than the customer's plan— or his actual results—we can plan improvement.

"According to our model of the optimal layout for a growth print shop of your volume and type of production," 3M can say, "your proposed layout departs from our optimum in ways that can deprive you of up to $1.5 million in profits over your first 30 months of operation."

"According to our model of an optimal receivables collection system for a mature food processor with your distribution channels," AT&T can say, "you can improve the profit contribution of your current system by an average of $500,000 a year."

Hewlett-Packard sales representatives walk along the manufacturing lines of a pharmaceutical company and say, "Our model design for automating a process like yours can help you reduce up to $200,000 in labor. According to our standards, your manning is excessive by five workers. Your control process is also slower than our standard in spotting and alerting you to deviations from specification. This will be reflected in added costs for quality assurance, scrap, and downtime. You can avoid these costs by computerizing your product testing and quality assurance. The difference between our models in these areas and your operations can yield you about three quarters of a million dollars in your first startup year."

A specialist's models announce what is special about him: he knows how to improve the profits of certain types of businesses at certain phases of their life cycles. He knows the standard specifications of what their profit values can be at each phase. He is the keeper of the norms for their industry—indeed, he is probably the discoverer and maker of many of them. If a customer exceeds these norms, the specialist can help maintain customer superiority. If the norms are better than customer profit performance, he can help bring the customer up to norm.

The Two Basic Proposal Models

The specialist sells from his norms. To do so, he must possess two basic models, one for new businesses and the other for mature businesses. The New Business Model must be segmented into three submodels: one for startup businesses, another for businesses making market entry, and the third for businesses undergoing fast growth. The content of these models is outlined in Figure 1-1 in Chapter 1.

A supplier's models are his stock in trade. He sells by superimposing them over models of customer businesses. A startup customer's model may be only a plan. It does not matter. The plan contains a pro forma financial projection of the business-to-be. This is its *As-If model:* as if it were up and running. The specialist's model is an *If-Then model:* if the customer adopts the specialist's model, then the customer's model will more nearly approach the specialist's model. The customer will become, or remain, improved.

The specialist does not sell his models. He sells the improved profits that his models propose.

A model highlights customer profits. It says that there is a better way than the customer is currently practicing. The profit difference between the customer's way and the specialist's model represents the added value of the specialist. If, for example, he can enable a startup to enter its market one day earlier than planned, the dollar value of that day's earnings and the advance of one day in achieving payback of the startup's funding represent the specialist's added value.

The first thing that we as specialists should propose to a customer is our model for his business. If your business can approach my model, we can say, then the added values representing the differences between them will be yours. Do you want the added values?

What we say—Do you want the added values of these incremental profits?—is as important as what we do not say. We do not say, Do you want my product, service, or system? Nor do we say, Do you want my solution? We ask only if the customer wants his business to more closely resemble our model.

When we ask that question, we are proposing to sell. When the customer asks *how* he can make his business resemble our model, the customer is proposing to buy.

A Model Proposal

If improving the profit contribution from startups is our specialty, we must know how a business can avoid costs and ensure sales even before it goes commercial. This puts us in a unique position. No company expects profits from its startups. Quite the opposite—startups are cost centers. Not until growth can they be profitmakers. Yet we can improve a startup's contribution to profits by accelerating its growth in two ways. We can help it avoid costs it would otherwise incur, thereby either reducing the funds required to sponsor it or allowing them to be reallocated. And we can help the startup avoid the cost of misidentifying its heavy-profit contributing market or underestimating the maximum price that the market will pay.

We can say, We know your industry, and we specialize in it. We know the standard problems that a new business can incur in some of its major operating functions in this industry. Each of these problems carries a direct cost. If you incorporate these standard problems into your business, you will build their unnecessary costs into its operations. They will adversely affect your quality assurance, your productivity, and your planned date for market entry. We also know the standard opportunities for a startup business in your industry. If you miss out on them, or on achieving them fully, you will be leaving money on the table. Entry will be prolonged. It will take longer and cost more to begin growth. You may never make it big.

Models are numerical, not verbal. A model does not say to a customer that we can improve his profits "a lot" without being able to measure them. A model does not say to a customer that we can improve his profits "soon." There is no space on a customer's profit and loss statement to show "a lot" of profit. Nor is there a planning time frame called "soon." Models exist in dollar values and time values or they do not exist at all. There is a simple reason for this. Profits exist in dollars over time or they do not exist at all.

A model is composed of two sets of numbers: the dollar

value of customer profits, and the time value of these profits. Dollars are meaningless unless they are related to the time when they will be realized. A dollar in hand is worth several dollars in the bush. This is because a dollar today is always worth more than the same dollar tomorrow. In between, today's dollar can be appreciated by investment. Today's dollar, plus its overnight invested value, will always exceed the value of the same dollar by itself tomorrow.

Because models are preoccupied with answering *how much?* and *how soon?* they appear as financial statements of invested costs and the profit benefits that are returned from them. They could be called investment-return models. More often they are known as cost-benefit models, where the costs are regarded as investments that yield the benefits that are to be returned. Because the costs result in a return, they are true investments.

Figure 5-1 shows a model cost-benefit analysis. It compares a customer's incremental investment with the incremental rate of return that it will yield. To arrive at the return, the costs of doing things the customer's current way are compared against the benefits of the supplier's proposal. The results are expressed in two ways the customer can understand: net income and rate of return. Figure 5-1 is a one-year analysis. To make it relevant to a five-year time frame, the year-by-year cash flow would have to be shown. Each year's flow beyond year one would have to be discounted to disclose its present value, which would be approximately 10 percent less each year due to the time value of money.

A business model like this is an incomparably potent sales tool because it can induce the two customer reactions that predispose penetration. The first is *agreement* that the customer has a problem or an opportunity. Without agreement, nothing happens. If we are alone in perceiving a problem, we will be left with both our perception and our product. The second reaction engendered by the business model is customer desire for *the solution*—not *a solution,* not *any solution,* but *the solution* represented in the model as the industry standard.

Figure 5-1. **Cost-benefit analysis.**

Incremental Investment

1. Cost of proposed equipment/system $_____
2. Installation costs   +_____
3. Investment in other assets required   +_____
4. Avoidable costs (repairs & remodeling)   −_____
5. Net after-tax adjustment for sale of properties retired as a result of investment   −_____
6. Total Investment   =========

Costs-Benefits (Annual Basis)

	Proposal	Present or Competitive	+ − Difference
7. Sales revenue	$_____	$_____	$_____
Variable Costs:			
8. Labor (including fringe benefits)	_____	_____	_____
9. Materials	_____	_____	_____
10. Maintenance	_____	_____	_____
11. Other variable costs	_____	_____	_____
12. Total variable costs	_____	_____	_____
13. Contribution margin (7 − 12)	_____	_____	_____
Fixed Costs:			
14. Rent or depreciation on equipment	_____	_____	_____
15. Other fixed costs	_____	_____	_____
16. Total fixed costs	_____	_____	_____
17. Net income before taxes	_____	_____	_____

Accounting Rate of Return on Proposed Investment

18. Total investment cost (6 or total capitalized annual cost of system) $_____
19. Net income before taxes for year (17) $_____
20. Before-tax rate of return (19 ÷ 18)   ___%

In addition to their roles as penetration tools, business models also position us in the two most important ways that anyone who sells can represent himself. Our models prove that we have *experience* in the customer's business. Our experience is more than with the customer's business in general. It is with the specific phase of the customer's life cycle that is most relevant to him right now.

Our models also prove something else about us. Because we can affect the normal costs that our experience has taught us exist at each life-cycle phase, we possess the *expertise* to do the same in the customer's business. By combining experience and expertise as the basic platform of our position, we can convey our industry leadership without the self-serving need to proclaim it. Proclaiming leadership is the province of vendors, who must testify for themselves because their customers will not do it for them.

Models limit the customer's options to procrastinate. They constrain his desire to seek out competitive suppliers. By selling from models, we can outdistance ourselves from competition. Our experience and expertise help us do this. If the customer deliberates too long, debating whether there is a better or cheaper way of approaching the industry standard or someone easier to work with, he incurs opportunity cost. While he ponders, he could be improving his profits. Even if he finds someone else who eventually improves his bottom line to a greater degree or less expensively, he may never make up the time value of the profits he has surrendered by delay.

We can gain insight into how customers' minds work when they contemplate our proposals by learning how they calculate incremental profit and how they approve capital expenditures. The processes they use to evaluate what we offer and to assess its impact on their businesses are revealed in Appendixes A and B.

Proposing with a Startup-Phase Model

A startup-phase model must be based primarily on cost avoidance in preparing for market entry. Secondarily, it can be based on preventing sales opportunity loss.

Before it makes market entry, a new business is a collection of sunk costs. While its asset base is being planned and laid down, nothing is available for sale. Hence, its cash flow is negative. The capital funds that have been appropriated for it are being invested at a high rate of expenditure. Everything is going out, nothing is coming in.

How many of these costs can be avoided? Every dollar saved at this point is worth more than a dollar earned later. A dollar that can be saved can be immediately invested elsewhere. Or it can be returned to the startup's sponsor, lowering the total investment and, by reducing the eventual breakeven point, speeding payback.

Startup models are heavily into cost displacement or cost replacement. They wipe out a cost category or consolidate several costs into a single lower cost. They substitute a less costly solution, such as automation, for a more costly investment, such as human labor. The total of what they save can be regarded as the equivalent of profits from sales that cannot yet be made.

The second area of startup model concentration is on reducing the threat of incurring opportunity costs that can delay market entry or can come back to haunt a business after it has been commercialized. These opportunity areas typically involve four business functions: (1) market analysis, to make sure the market is rightly assessed from the start; (2) product and process design, to make sure that the product is right and is manufactured cost-effectively; (3) quality assurance, to make sure that the product will not incur excessive warranty costs for repair or costs for replacement or recall; and (4) forecasting and inventory control, to make sure that the product is neither backordered, causing lost sales, nor overstocked, causing excessive handling, storage, and insurance costs.

Proposing with an Entry-Phase Model

An entry-phase model must be based primarily on generating sales and secondarily on preventing the further loss of sales opportunities.

Immediately on its market entry, a business presses for breakeven. This is the milestone that signals the payback of its founding investment. In order to achieve continuing growth, the business must focus on maximizing revenues and earnings.

How many more incremental sales dollars can be brought in? How much faster can they be booked? How much faster can they be collected and converted into receipts? In other words, how fast can the market be penetrated, how fully and completely can its opportunity be capitalized, and how great a percentage of total sales can be realized?

Every qualified customer who remains unsold represents an opportunity cost. Every customer who buys one unit but could have bought two represents opportunity cost. Every customer who leases instead of buys may also represent opportunity cost.

Entry models must pay equal attention to internal factors that can influence the outflow of product and the inflow of revenue. Forecasting and inventory must be attuned to the market's drive. Quality must be maintained. Downtime must be minimized lest it cut off the flow of marketable products. These business functions must be treated as sales aids, not contributors to cost. At entry, as in growth, direct costs are comparatively irrelevant.

Proposing with a Growth-Phase Model

A growth-phase model must be primarily based on accelerating the sales that begin with entry. It must also be concerned with preventing the opportunity cost of lost sales.

The growth phase has two objectives. The first is to maximize market entry by selling up to the full manufacturing capacity of the business. This puts the emphasis on gaining market share as quickly as possible and driving the growth curve as high as it can go. A growth business has an insatiable appetite. It devours cash. Therefore, cash flow must be insured. It is a cardinal sin to lose sales because lack of cash or capacity prevents their fulfillment. This means that productivity must be maintained, with its quality tightly controlled. Nothing suffocates growth like the inability to get products out the door except the inability to keep them from coming back.

How much faster can the business be grown? How much faster can inventory be turned and receivables collected? How can downtime be minimized and quality maintained?

The second objective of the growth phase is to prepare the business for its next entry. A successful market entry not only justifies proliferation, it demands it. Market acceptance offers opportunity for market expansion.

How cost-effectively can a second entry follow on the growth of its pathfinder? What economies can be gained by sharing asset bases? How can the initial product's reputation for quality be bred into the next product? How can tie-in sales create a system for selling the first and second products together?

The transcendent dedication of a growth model must be to perpetrate growth. How long can a growth rate of sales and profitmaking be maintained? Since growth is a rate and not a state, this is the key question for growth modeling. Every additional day that the rate of growth can be sustained is an added day of premium profits—one day more during which the onset of the declining margins of maturity can be postponed.

Proposing with a Mature-Phase Model

A mature-phase model must be primarily based on delaying the decline of profit per sale that is the inevitable result of the end-point of growth. Even though volume at maturity may be huge, decaying margins and increasing costs absorb revenues at a stepped-up rate as maturity progresses. The mature phase of a business, therefore, requires a delicate balance between maintaining or increasing sales and maintaining or decreasing costs, including the cost of sales. The expansion of sales comes harder in mature markets, where the markets themselves are not growing and increased penetration requires the conquest of a portion of a competitor's share. How can sales be increased cost-effectively? How can sales be maintained more economically? How can the product be renovated marginally to provide a sales incentive, yet keep costs down? How can costs—any costs, all costs—be better controlled?

Mature models focus heavily on productivity improvement as a means of increasing output at lower or equal cost. By the time a business becomes mature, its assets have become a mixed blessing. They provide the business with a capability base, but they also represent costs. Can the asset base be reduced? Can it be modernized? Can it be made more productive? Buying instead of making, leasing instead of buying, operating jointly instead of going it alone—all these can provide alternatives to cost.

Just as growth models are dedicated to perpetuating the growth phase, mature models must perpetuate maturity as long as possible. How long can the business yield an acceptable rate of return on its assets before the assets become more valuable than their return? This is the key question for mature modeling. Every additional day that the return from a mature business can be sustained at an acceptable rate is an added day of cash flow and market presence—one day more during which downsizing or divestiture has been postponed.

Business with mature customers is bought as much as it is sold. Even a winner may not make much money by penetrating a mature customer when his cost of sales is subtracted from his constrained margins. A supplier can move goods, generate cash flow, and make the news; but he will probably forsake significant profits per unit as the price of this kind of success.

How can mature customers be proposed to so that customers and their suppliers will make money? Two strategies for off–balance-sheet financing may provide the answers.

Cash-Flow Financing, Fees, and Leases

Through cash-flow financing, fees, and leases, a customer's profits can be improved while he has use of the supplier's product—in effect, allowing him to have his cake and eat it, too.

There are three basic methods of large-purchase financing:

1. *Cash-flow financing*—payments are related to depreciation so that products can pay for themselves.
2. *Monthly service fee*—time payments are made until the price is paid in full.
3. *Lease*—either a perpetual rental basis or an eventual conversion to purchase.

Under leasing, a customer never takes ownership. A lump-sum cost for outright purchase is avoided. Cash and borrowing power are conserved. For customers who are already borrowed up to their credit limit or, conversely, who want to keep their borrowing power unimpaired, leasing is an ideal arrangement. Leasing can also be the option of choice if a supplier's technology is new and will probably be improved, or if competitive suppliers are selling on price and offering unusually liberal financing terms.

Joint Venture

Another form of off–balance-sheet financing for a mature customer is the creation of a third entity, a joint venture between supplier and customer. This new business can be organized to carry out the customer's intended function, much like spinning it out as a separate going concern. For example, a joint venture can act as an information processing company to handle all of a customer's data processing and telecommunications needs. The venture, and not the parent company, acquires the supplier's computers and software, as well as its service, technical, and maintenance support. The supplier upgrades his products over time, guaranteeing that state-of-the-art equipment is always on line. To encourage its full use, the supplier may even provide sales, advertising, and marketing assistance to the customer through their venture.

One potential sharing arrangement for a joint venture of this type may be a structure in which the supplier owns, say, 81 percent of the voting stock. In this way, the joint venture is consolidated on the supplier's books, while the customer has only a one-line balance sheet entry: "Minority Investment in Joint Venture." The supplier writes a finance lease to the joint venture, which in turn makes monthly payments back to the supplier. The joint venture bundles operating lease payments plus charges for technical, marketing, and other services into one lump-sum billing to the customer. In turn, the customer can invoice and collect from its operating units that use the system and repay the joint venture. The customer recognizes no income from the joint venture unless a dividend is paid.

Other shared arrangements between supplier and customer are also possible, ranging from supplier ownership of 51 percent of the joint venture, equal ownership, or 49 percent or less.

Proposing without Product

What is it like not to have a product to talk about? At first, we will feel naked. After all, the product is the seller's traditional refuge. Without the familiar security blanket of the features and benefits that we have come to know so well, we have no choice but to attend to the focal point of the customer's attention—his business, his business functions, and their contributions to his business profit. At last, we and our customers can share the same priorities.

What will we say about the customer's business? Once we know its life-cycle mode, we can talk knowledgeably about it in these four areas:

1. Where the major costs are bound to be and how much they normally contribute.

2. Where the major opportunities are bound to be and how much they normally can contribute.

3. Where we can help and, when we do, how much cost reduction and how much sales increase typically results.

4. What our best conservative estimate suggests about the cost reductions and sales increases that we can generate for the customer.

By the time we get to the fourth item, we will no longer be talking alone. The customer will begin to talk, opening the dialog with us by asking the magic question, "How?" *How* can we find out *how much* the true value of our improvement can be and, if it is significant to us once we find out, *how soon* can we get it?

By asking *how,* the customer will open our sale. By answering *how much* and *how soon,* he will close it.

If we drive our sales with our product, we will have to penetrate by asking the customer, in one way or another, to take the product off our hands. We will also have to close our sales. When the customer drives our sales, he does both jobs for us. Our job comes in between, when we answer the question *How?*

How is the acid test. It tests our expertise and our ability to apply it. Without applications capability, expertise is academic. By letting the customer drive our sales, we spend our selling time talking about our most priceless possession—not our product, but our ability to apply it to improve the profit of our customer's business.

The profit results of applying our expertise should be our favorite subject. We should talk about it every chance we have. What else will consistently differentiate us? What else will demonstrate to the customer how and how much we can help him? Certainly not our product. In and of itself, it is an inert cost. Only when our product is applied with expertise does it come alive, taking on meaning by its contribution to customer profits.

Guaranteeing Improved Profits

The value-seller knows his norms. Based on them, he can propose with certainty: At this phase of your life cycle, we can expect to improve your profit within our normal range of 5 to 9 percent which, in your case, translates conservatively into $500,000 over the next 12 months.

In this way, the seller has quantified his value in two of its essential three terms. He has answered the question, *How much*. He has also answered *How soon*. To clinch the deal, he must now attest to the certainty of his proposal. How sure can the customer be that he will receive the full amount of improved profit on time?

Any transaction in which money is exchanged puts a premium on certainty. Once a customer has been promised incremental profits, he must receive them because he will already have planned their immediate investment. Every day they are delayed incurs opportunity cost. If the delay is protracted, the entire opportunity may vanish. Of the three specifications of money—quantity, time, and certainty—the most important is certainty. Without it, the other two become meaningless. The time value of money will deprive them of meaning.

Improved profits that cannot be counted cannot be planned for investment. Profits that cannot be planned have no reality. In effect, they do not exist. Proposing nonexistent profits is an exercise in futility.

How confident are we that we can deliver new profits to a customer within our norms? This is the acid test of our ability as a profit-improver. If we cannot be confident, we cannot penetrate customer businesses as a value-adder. If, on the other hand, we are confident, not only can we perform as we propose, we can *guarantee* it.

Nothing is more powerful than a guaranteed Profit Improvement Proposal. It demonstrates the seller's conviction. It soothes the customer's need for comfort. It makes the seller's norms truly the standard of the customer's industry. It bonds supplier and customer to a shared reward.

Because it shares the risk as no other commitment can do, the performance bond guarantees partnership. No longer is the customer the sole worrier. The supplier now shares his concern. The customer's inherent risk, which is always greater than his supplier's when he permits intrusions, discontinuities, and alterations in his operations, is smoothed. He is now assured of gain.

The customer wants his full proposed profits. The supplier must deliver them. If he cannot make them occur from the impact he has on the customer's business, he must make up the difference between what he has proposed and what has actually been achieved.

A supplier who guarantees results in this way takes a stand behind his norms. He asserts in the penultimate manner that he knows his value. One way or the other, he will provide it. Knowing in advance that any shortfall will be his to make up, he will tend to be properly conservative in his profit proposals. He will be more realistic about what it takes to make things happen in a customer's business. He will do his homework with greater diligence and make more concerted use of his customer data, whose importance he will come to cherish. He will be more believable to his customers, because they will know all these things about him and so will be able to place greater trust and confidence in his contribution to their partnership.

In addition to its partnering effect on the customer, guaranteed profit performance has a deterrent effect on the supplier's competitors. They now have an added problem. If they cannot also guarantee their value, they lose competitiveness. If they try to reciprocate, they will be risking outrageous odds because they lack the incumbent's privileged knowledge of his customer's business. Just as getting in becomes easier, so does staying in. Not only has penetration occurred. It has closed the door behind itself.

6

Branding the Benefits

Earning Premium Margins for Adding Life-Cycle Values

Branding is the strategy of user differentiation. By enriching our customers, we differentiate them. We give them new wealth that enhances them and makes them stand out from their competitors. We make them "best." Or we give them new power that enables them to control their personal or business life styles, make them more productive and predictable, and allow them to reward those who depend on them. We brand them with the twin cachets of success: richness and distinction.

In the process, we brand ourselves as different, too. We are no longer one of several alternate vendors, each with a parity product whose only true variation is price. We are growers. As such, we can tell a branded customer when we see one. Someone is growing him by improving his profit. We can tell when we are branded, too. We are being grown by our customers. They are paying us a premium unit price.

There are, accordingly, two definitions of branding. The customer's definition says that branding is the profit difference between his business and the competition. The supplier's definition says that branding is the ability to command premium price by conferring premium profit on customers—in other words, the profit difference between his business and the competition. For both customers and their suppliers, branding is the same.

Branders and Values

Branders deal in values, not products. To say the same thing in another way, brander's products are not physical, tangible hardware, but physical, tangible profits for their customers. Branders sell money—new money that their customers would not have available to them without a brand partnership. Instead of asking, How can we sell this customer, branders ask, How can we grow him? How can we add value to his business? How can we improve his profits?

Customer-Specific Values

Unlike vendors, each of whose products bears an off-the-shelf price, branders originate price with each customer. This means that no price can be placed on a brander's value until the value has been calculated for a customer's business. Each value is customer-specific. As a result, branders do not publish a price list, nor do they sell products from a catalog.

On the shelf, a brander's products represent only costs. If these costs were simply transferred to customers in the form of price, the brander would become a vendor. Instead, *branders create value*. Partly through the performance of their products, partly through their knowledge of customers and their applications expertise, branders come into the businesses of their customers and create values that were not there before. When they are finished, their customers have greater worth.

There is no way to value a brander exclusive of his performance. That is why proof of performance is so vital to branding: especially proof of a track record and proof in the form of a cost-benefit analysis that shows how the track record can be applied to a specific customer's business. This accounts for the highly personal, individualistic relationship that each customer has with a brander.

Even though the brander serves many customers in the same industry, he creates different values for each of them. Customers who have never worked as partners with a brander may ask him, Will you do the same thing for my competitors? If by "the same thing" the customer means will the brander improve competitor profits, the answer is *yes*. But the answer is *no* if he is asking if all competitors will have their profits improved in the same amount within the same time at the same degree of certainty. If that were the case, the brander would be a vendor.

Branders leave their customers no choice but to value them on the values they create. These values come from a brander's systems when they become operational within a customer's business. The brander enters a customer's manufacturing function, for example, reduces the cost of a process, and creates a new value. Or he enters a customer's marketing function, increases the sales revenues from a market, and creates a new value. The new values that are created have been planned in advance. There are no surprises. The brander has based his price on them. The customer has based his value-to-price relationship on them. He has already planned how to reinvest the new values. Some portion of the value he reinvests may be with the brander, so that another cycle of profit improvement can be initiated; in vendor terms, the customer will reorder.

In such an event, the customer is no longer playing with his own money. He is using incremental funds that the brander has created for him—money that does not have to be drawn off from operating funds or reallocated from other priorities. This may be the greatest value that a brander provides.

Putting a Value on the Value

No matter how much a brander learns about the business of his customers, they know one thing that he must discover anew with every transaction. The brander knows how much value he can add. Only the customer can put a value on the value; only the customer can tell the brander what his value will be worth. A brander can say, I can improve your profits by $100,000. It is up to his customer to say, That will be worth $250,000 to me in 18 months.

A customer will always set a value that is higher than a brander's face value. Branders deal in applied value. Customers take *applied value* and multiply it to its second derivative, investment value. They calculate its *investment value* based on what they plan to do with the applied value. They may invest it in their own business, or they may invest it outside. Either way, they will use it for growth. The net worth of that growth will be the customer's concept of true value.

In business, value is used to beget value. Money makes money. Circulation of capital depends on the turnover principle for the velocity by which value is generated (see Appendix A for a full explanation of turnover.) The more money that can be circulated, the greater the multiplier effect of turnover can be. Branders affect both components of the capital circulatory system. They bring more money into the system, and they help customers turn it over faster by providing premier opportunities for investment.

It is the customer's invested value—what it will amount to when it is calculated as "future value"—and not the brander's applied value that should be the basis of brand price. (See Appendix B for a full explanation of calculating value.)

Future value is the total value that will accrue as the result of a present investment. Time is therefore of the essence. The faster the brander can create values in customer businesses, the sooner customers can invest them to make more. For this reason—because money exists only in the context of time—there can be no consideration of dollar values without time values.

Long time frames without payout devalue money, just as short time frames enrich it. The brander's definition of *what* he sells—money—is never complete without his definition of *when* it will become available for use.

Vendors are constrained to deliver their product values on time. So are branders. For them, being on time involves more than having physical products on a customer's receiving dock. It means having new dollars in the customer's till. This is the function of the brander's application skill. Nothing happens to make a customer more profitable just because a shipping date is met. That simply transfers a cost from supplier to customer. Until a customer's business functions are affected—until a brander's appliers make their applications and a cost is reduced or sales revenues are increased—value remains to be seen.

Because the brander's value is applications value, it is clear that a brander is beholden to his application experts. He is entirely in their hands. They hold his brand posture. They control his effectiveness as a brander. They determine whether he is a brander or a vendor in disguise.

When customers buy brands, they are really buying a brander's applications experts—his teams of consultative account representatives and their technical, financial, and data-support staffs. No brander can be better than his experts. No matter how heavily capitalized a brander may be, branding is a labor-intensive business. Capital cannot apply itself; only people can apply it. Capital cannot create partnerships with customer function managers; only people can partner. Capital, even in the form of product values, cannot brand; only people can brand the customer values on which branding depends.

The Futility of Branding Product Values

The cycle of investment and reinvestment of the brander's values is unique to branding. It is impossible to accomplish with product values alone. This is why vendors must make every sale all over again, as if it were the first sale. They lack inherent continuity because they cannot quantify the customer values, if any, that their products contribute. They pay the price for seeking to differentiate their products instead of their customers.

To the same extent that branders are obsessed with their customers and making them into winners, vendors are obsessed with their competitors and making them into losers.

Branders try to enhance the objects of their obsession; vendors try to diminish them. To do this, they enhance themselves, their products, and the processes by which they are made.

Secret or exclusive ingredients, magic formulas, and exotic formulations—"contented cows" from Borden's and the father-and-son assembly teams of Studebaker—have historically been invoked by vendors to distinguish their parity products from all others. Continental Can's "Econoweld" was American Can's "Miraseam"; each welds tin-free steel cans seamlessly. Each adds value to the product. But what is the value added to the customer? Unless there is an answer to this question, each will have to be sold on product value. If both products turn out to be equally valued, price will be equal, too.

In the past half century, only two major manufacturers have been successfully branded on the basis of product value. One was Xerox; the other was Polaroid. For approximately a generation each commanded a brand price. But neither could prove a unique customer value to support a brand price when less expensive competition ended their honeymoons. They became commodities virtually overnight. Neither has ever fully recovered.

Because brand values are customer values, no one covets them more than customers themselves. In contrast, only vendors covet their product values. They explain them through infinite detail, exhibit them in closeup microphotographs and cutaway drawings, and exalt them in purple prose. When they finish, customers ask the inevitable question, How much? Whatever the vendors reply, customers say, Too much. The only way that customers can create added value is to reduce the vendor's added cost, his price.

Forms of Enriched Value

The value that a brander can add to customers may take three forms. The most straightforward form is *improved profits*. They are always desirable, preferable by far to any other value by a profitmaking business. They are advantageous for two other reasons as well. Profits can be accurately measured and immediately invested. They are the closest a customer can come to instant growth. This is equally true for the brander, since his customer's profits—because they are quantifiable— can be premium priced.

A second form of customer value is *improved productivity,* which is specifically important to nonprofit and not-for-profit customers. Improved productivity provides incremental performance advantages. People and functions operate more cost-effectively. Either more output results from the same asset base or a smaller, reduced asset base yields the same output. Productivity can be measured, although not as precisely as profits, but it cannot always be translated into a value. Operating more cost-effectively is an acceptable objective if growth is to be achieved through cost reduction. Productivity brings costs down. Growth, however, depends on more than just elevated productivity. It depends on developing a demand base for the added capacity. Otherwise, productivity gains lead to unanswerable questions such as, How do we utilize the one-third of a man we have just freed up?

A third value is *improved pride.* It can be neither measured nor invested. Nonetheless, it can be demonstrated in such business attributes as heightened incentive, better morale, and even greater productivity. While feeling good and working well are not necessarily the same thing, feeling good may help reduce absenteeism, turnover, rejects, and callbacks. This, in turn, may improve profits. Affecting pride alone is a brander's weakest position. But pride value is a worthwhile additive to productivity value. Two unmeasurables do not add up to strength, but their reinforcing effect on each other may accomplish what neither alone can do: help brand a customer and merit a premium reward for the brander.

Maximizing the Value Market

Branders can add value to any business whose costs they can reduce or whose sales revenues they can increase. By applying their expertise and systems to customer operations where they are process-smart and to customers' customers where they are market-smart, branders can grow their value. Because brand growth is customer-specific, some customers can be grown more than others. These are the customers whom the brander can enrich the most. They are also the same customers who have the greatest capability to enrich the brander. The scarcity of applications expertise, the absorbing demands imposed by partnering, and the time pressure to add values fast make it necessary for branders to concentrate. Where can they maximize their value-adding potential?

Within the brander's natural constituencies of growing and growable customers, brand strategy must vary with customer positioning. There are three basic positions in which a brander will find his customers. Two of them compose his best market for value. They help him maximize his contribution and his resulting reward.

First are the young entrepreneur companies in a fast-growth mode. They can use all the added value they can get. The form in which it is most desirable to them will be added sales revenues. Growth businesses race the clock. They need to strike while the volume is hot, before competitors can mature them or an innovative technology can preempt them. They need money to manufacture, money to market, and money to expand. Because they are growing at a high rate, a brander can help them significantly by adding even a single percentage point to their growth.

The second category of prime candidates is well-established mature businesses that are in decline but are still growable. Unlike new growth companies for whom cost reduction is almost irrelevant as a growth strategy, mature businesses can be grown by reducing their costs as well as by increasing their market share. Since their asset base is already bought and paid for and usually has underutilized capacity, incremental sales will add little incremental cost. They will be highly profitable. Any reduction in business-function costs will further reduce the asset-base burden, amplifying profits even more.

A large corporation will have many businesses that can be grown or regrown. If they have the same business functions that the brander can affect, he can add value by cost reduction for multiple customers under the same roof. If some of them serve the same markets, he can help them add sales revenues as well.

A business in the third position, stability, is neither growing nor is it likely to be growable. It is therefore not a candidate for branding. Stable businesses are static. They possess none of the dynamic instability of new growth or mature rejuvenation. New and mature businesses must grow. They have no alternative. If they cannot grow, new businesses will become mature and mature businesses will become extinct. Stable businesses, on the other hand, must remain stable. If they were to destabilize themselves with an unreturnable investment or an unproductive—even worse, a backfiring—market strategy, the loss would be unrecoverable. They would plunge into decline.

Instead of living in the hope of expansive growth, stable businesses live with the specter of decline. The chance to grow—to be branded—is not worth the risk of decline: probable risk is greater than potential reward. Invitations to grow will be reacted to slowly, rationalized to a faretheewell (Can it work *here?*), and eventually rejected. Only when a stable business finally declines will it become a qualified candidate for branding.

Taking a Branded Posture

While vendors are praising themselves and condemning their competitors, branders are partnering with customers. Vendors try to isolate themselves from their lookalikes. Branders try to ally themselves with growth partners, the customers whose growth will determine their own. But branders cannot simply legislate partnerships, nor can they grow someone else's business uninvited. They must first demonstrate their capabilities. What are the base abilities of branding? There are three: the ability *to apply growth* to a customer, the ability *to teach growth* to a customer, and the ability *to prove growth* to a customer.

Authority on Applications

A brander must posture himself as the applications authority in the customer's industry. This is his prior certification.

Applications authority presumes two capabilities. One is a knowledge of the customer's business: knowing the *what* about a customer. The second is a knowledge of implementation: the *how* about installing a product or system in a customer's operations. To know the *what* without the *how* is to be an academic. To attempt the *how* without knowing the *what* is like do-it-yourself brain surgery.

In order to be an expert at applying a product or system to a customer's business functions, a brander must be skilled at four things:

1. He must have entry skills so he can penetrate an operating process at the proper point, one of the 20 percent of its cost clusters or sales opportunities that yield 80 percent of the results.
2. He must have installation skills so he can integrate his product or system with a customer's ongoing operations, disrupting them minimally.
3. He must have migration skills so he can progressively improve a customer's operations by adding to them new products or services or an upgraded system.
4. He must have measurement skills so he can prove that the customer's productivity and profits are being increased according to plan.

There is no escape from application. That is what a brander is paid for. Without application, profits can only be talked. Application can make them happen. The ability to put expertise to work, to install it together with a product or service system in a customer's business and make profits as a result, is the brander's artistry. It defines his relationship with customers. It answers the question, Why do business with the high-priced supplier? It reminds the brander what business he is in and directs his attention and resources to his true assets—knowledgeable people.

Authority on Education

A brander must also posture himself as the education authority in the customer's industry. This is his companion certification to applications authority.

An applier who can demonstrate that he improves customer profit will be sought after on two grounds. One will be invitations to apply himself to other customer businesses—to do for them what he has demonstrated he can do for others. The other will be invitations to teach customer people how to internalize the brander's expertise.

How can a customer's work force keep down the costs that the brander can reduce? How can they maintain improved productivity, suppress downtime, keep receivables collected, forecast more exactingly, or balance inventory more optimally? How can they keep up the sales revenues that the brander can increase—how can they continue to grow their own customers, substantiate premium prices, and concentrate on doing business with high-level decision-makers?

Branders must be more than good appliers. They must also be good teachers of how application must be made to ensure improved profits. If they cannot teach, they will have no multiplier of their ability to make a financial impact on customer businesses. As soon as they have finished their application, the value of their contribution will begin an immediate decline as customers regain control of their enhanced business functions. Operationally, these functions would be demonstrably better. But as profit-improvers, they would quickly diminish in effectiveness over time.

Training not only accelerates a customer's learning curve, it helps guarantee that there will be one. It gives a customer proprietorship of his systems for improving profit: they become "his" and not the brander's. As customers become trained in improving their profits, they can put a knowledgeable value on their partnership with the brander. They will want to protect and preserve it. More importantly, they will want to grow it. Once having experienced the value of an incremental dollar, they will want more.

So important is the brander's need to be a training authority that teaching and learning must be the cyclical rhythm of his partnerships. He must teach what he knows. He must learn the rest. The more he teaches, the more he will learn; every solution reveals the next problem. The more he learns, the more opportunity he will find to teach. What he learns will compose his database. What he teaches will compose his proposals to improve customer profits.

The brand relationship begins with teaching. The brander's initial approach to a customer is based on sharing something the brander knows. It may be something quite specific about the customer's business. Or it may be a generality, a norm, about the customer's industry in a category where the brander believes the customer to be deficient.

From that moment on, the brander is always in a teaching role. He constantly brings new information to the surface: look at what is going on in this or that operation; look at our progress in improving its contribution. He counsels on what options for improvement exist and recommends the option of choice: Go with this one because it represents the optimal solution. He audits, analyzes, and reviews results, making lessons clear and drawing up an operational curriculum so that the customer's old hands can be reinforced and new hires informed about the whys and wherefores of what he has done.

Branders build monuments in their customer businesses.

They are not systems. They are people—customer people who take over the brander's skills and thereby free him to concentrate on new problems and again begin to apply and educate, teach and learn.

Authority on Proof

Branders do not say, Trust me. Take my word. They say, Partner me. Take my profits. They do not ask for acts of faith. They present acts of proof. Adept at quantifying their results, branders put numbers on their contributions so that the significance of each contribution can be judged. Is the brander doing his job? Is he earning his premium pay? The proof is in the profits. Is the brander's contribution still coming in? Was he just a one-time hotshot? The proof is in the profits. What is the brander worth to us? How can we get a fix on his true value? The proof is in the profits.

A brander's norms arm him with proof of what he can do. They give conjecture some boundaries. But branders must prove something more than what they have done. They must prove they are doing it anew with each customer. And they must prove it each time. Because branders ask premium prices, they live in the world of "what have you done for me lately?" The customer will always consider his investment to be too high unless the return is always higher.

The brander's best friend is his cost-benefit analysis of a customer's business. It shows the benefits in terms of incremental profit as a return on incremental investment. Here is where you are now, the cost-benefit analysis reveals. Here are your current costs or sales. Here is where you will be in return for this incremental investment. Here is your current bottom line: net profit before tax and rate of return. Here it is again after our proposal. This is the benefit, the value added by doing business with a brander.

The cost-benefit analysis proves the value of the brander's authoritativeness in applications expertise and his skill as an educator. It declares straightaway exactly how much of an authority he really is: not how much he knows, but how much of it he can pay off for the customer; not how much he knows, but how much of it he can teach the customer.

Branders are constantly required to provide four kinds of proof. First, before they can create a brand partnership, they must prove that they have a track record. They have already improved someone's profit, preferably in a customer's own industry or an industry to which he can relate. The best proof is the case history. Through customer testimonials, the brander's capabilities are proclaimed for him. Testimonials tell how customers have become "best" as a result of partnering with their branders. That is why when branders advertise, they never write a word of their own. Their customers speak for them. They speak in customer language, the only language that other customers understand. It is not the language of high-pressure sales persuasion. It is the language of high-level profit improvement.

After branders prove their track record, they enter the second stage of proof. As a result of applying their capabilities to solve customer problems and help seize customer opportunities, branders become smart. They become process-smart about customer cost problems and market-smart about customer sales opportunities. They learn average costs on a process-by-process basis. They learn the value of decreasing them by a single percentage point. They learn the average investment required and the return that can be expected. The same is true for sales. Branders learn the average dollar value of a market-share point on a market-by-market basis. They learn the value of increasing it by a single percentage point. They learn the average investment required and the return that can be expected. They must teach these industry averages—the brander's "norms"—to their customers to prove they know their industry.

Industry knowledge of and by itself, however, is never sufficient. The brander's third stage of proof must show customers why industry norms are important to them as yardsticks against which their own performance can be measured. Here is the average cost contributed by this business function in similar companies. Are you above it or below it? If you are below, what is it worth to raise it closer to the norm? If you invest that much to do it, what will be your return? Here is the average sales revenue contributed by this market segment for similar products. Are you above it or below it? If you are below, what is it worth to raise it closer to the norm? If you invest that much to do it, what will be your return?

What if a customer is above the norm? This gives him three options. He can leave well enough alone and go on to something else. He can safeguard his superiority. Or he can increase it even more, further improving its contribution to profit.

In this third stage of proof, the brander is showing customers that he knows something about their businesses. He knows where they are long on costs or short on sales revenues, either from his homework or from what they will teach him in response to his norms. He knows how to shorten the costs where they are long and to lengthen the sales revenues where they are short. Because he knows the customer's business and not just his own, he can earn the right to consult on its improvement.

The fourth and final stage of a brander's proof comes when he proves that he has a control system. It must progressively monitor the partners' progress in improving customer profit. It must also demonstrate that profit is being improved according to plan. We have done it successfully before. We have the industry norms as a result, and we know how your business compares against them. We can measure our ability to improve your performance. These are the proofs that branders must present to gain customer acceptance of their brand posture.

Armed with testimonials that fulfill the requirements for the first two stages of proof, plus a cost-benefit analysis that fulfills the last two stages, a brander is ready to take his position. Somewhere below him, "downstairs" in the customer hierarchy, a vendor who competes against the brander is presenting proof of his product's performance and warranty fulfillment. In this way, he too takes his position.

Brand Pricing

The price of a brand has five characteristics:

1. It is premium price.
2. It is compared with the improved profit it contributes to a customer's business, not to competitive prices.
3. It is recoverable by the customer's improved profit, eliminating price as a purchase decision.
4. It is not negotiable.
5. It varies in direct proportion to each customer's improved profit. This is the brand's "product." Since no two products are the same, no two prices can be the same.

These characteristics of brand price show how different it is from vendor pricing. This is because the effect of branding is to rule out price as the basis for purchase—the only basis that commodity selling has. Since a brand's purpose is to add value to its user—not to add a product to his inventory—brand price is attached to user value. It bears some proportion to its worth. The financial worth of the physical product or service that contributes to the customer's value is irrelevant. Its performance helps the customer achieve his added value. But it does not do so alone. Brand price does not reflect this partial contribution by being limited to product cost and nothing more. Instead, it is the consequence of the customer's total benefit.

In branding, price is not the cause of customer value; it is the result. Commodity selling makes price the cause, presenting a low price as creating customer value by lowering acquisition cost. With brand pricing, the customer's value is the financial value added by the brander. This *causes* price, which is positioned as the result of the customer's incremental worth.

Branding makes pricing customer-driven. It does not ask a customer what price he would like to pay or whether he thinks a certain price is fair. It asks what new value he needs to receive and what investment he is willing to make to obtain it. Brand price gives evidence of what a benefit is worth to the customer who will be rewarded by it. The customer's benefit is not *what we think it ought to be*. It is *what the customer thinks it is,* based on his valuation of a dollar's worth to him at the time when he does business with us.

In this manner, branders are relieved of the mystique of setting prices. Their customers set them as the prices of buying money—the price of capital, not capital goods. It is not a question of what the traffic will bear; it is what the traffic's growth is worth. Thus the brander is always on safe ground. The customer knows his growth objectives. He also knows what ratio of return to investment he can tolerate. Price, even premium price, will not be too high as long as the return it buys is commensurate with the customer's hurdle rate for investment: what a dollar of investment must clear to be considered a good deal.

Choosing Customer Confrontation

Price can be only one or the other: a cost or an investment. If price is positioned as a cost, it will confront a customer's cost-control system. The system is designed to reduce outside costs so that they can pass acceptably into customer operations without overwhelming them. This is the vendor's lot. He is perceived as a cost and must therefore be controlled.

When price is positioned as an investment, it escapes customer cost control. It now confronts a customer's profit-improvement system. This system is designed to increase earnings, generally from sales revenues. This is the brander's entry point. He is perceived as a profit improver and must therefore be encouraged.

To confront a customer's cost-control system is to sacrifice margins for volume. It is to forsake branding and accept the role of commodity vendor. No matter how small a supplier's margins may be, the apertures in the customer's cost-control system will be progressively reduced to deny them. On the other hand, when new profits instead of new costs are offered, they can never be too large. No matter how great they may be, the customer's profit-improvement system will always grow to accommodate them. It is possible for a customer to be unable to absorb a single added dollar of cost. But it is impossible not to be able to absorb new dollars of profit. This is how the brander becomes a preferential investment for his customers. He provides them with a preferential return. Customers buy to improve their profits. The more they buy, the more they improve them.

The return from a brander's price must meet three specifications that characterize any good investment. First, the return must meet or surpass the customer's hurdle rate for invested capital. Second, it must be forthcoming quickly enough to achieve early payback and begin positive cash flow. Third, it must not be reclaimed in whole or in part by later, followon costs.

In other words, first cost must be last cost, at least as far as significant expense is concerned. Initial price can be high as long as life-cycle costs are low. By "buying on price," the customer risks having hidden costs come back to haunt him and destroy the return on his original investment by adding to its expense without commensurately upgrading its yield. Costs of repairs outside warranty, downtime while repairs are made, and replacement if repairs are inadequate or too frequent are the bugaboos of price buying. So are product recalls and lawsuits for failure to deliver on time according to specifications.

A brand's "deal" with customers is that its high rate of return and low life-cycle costs merit a premium investment. Money in the bank, reliability of performance, and low or no offsetting costs have their value. Therefore they have their price.

The Brand Formula

A brand is a resolution of two forces. One is premium price. This is a brand's trademark. The other is premium value. This is a brand's "performance": what it does for its customers. These two variables must be in conjunction for branding to occur. The customer must receive a premium value in order to justify a premium price. The price can be high, even ultra-high, but the premium value must always exceed it.

The value-to-price relationship of a brand may be expressed as follows: Premium value must always be perceived to be greater than premium price.

$$\text{Perceived Premium Value} > \text{Premium Price}$$
$$\text{(PPV)} \qquad \text{(PP)}$$

The premium value of a brand is its return. It is the brand's yield, the incremental net worth that it confers on its user. Because this return comes about as a result of the investment made to acquire it, a brand's price is not a cost but an investment. A cost does not bear a positive incremental return. An investment does.

While brand pricing can be high, a high cost is acceptable only if it cannot be avoided. Costs are therefore compared against one another or against doing without. This is how commodities are bought and sold, in fierce competition. Investments, however, are compared against their returns. Comparing investments against each other on a dollar-for-dollar basis is inconclusive. The low investment may yield a disproportionately lower return than a high investment, making the latter the better buy.

Brand pricing is return-on-investment pricing. Brands ask for an investment, but they must sell its return. This is the value brands add, quantified in terms of their dollar value at the moment they fully accrue.

Asking Brand Questions

The single most crucial component of brand strategy is determining a brand's value-based price point. It will almost always be higher than we first dare. This is because we are limited in our knowledge. We know a brand's cost. Only its users know its value to them and therefore what they will pay to gain it.

We can now see clearly the three questions of utmost significance that we must ask of each potential brand:

1. *Who is its market*—who needs to have value added?
2. *What value will they receive*—how much added value will they benefit from?
3. *How much will it be worth to them*—what will they invest to achieve the added value?

The answer to the third question tells us the brand price. It comes from the answer to the second question, which tells us the brand value that is the basis for price. The answer to the second question is the brander's stock in trade. He must know the value he brings to his customers, not just the cost he represents. To be a brander means to be a value-bringer. It is not enough to know the nature of the value we bring, such as "lowered cost" or "added sales." We must know *how much and how soon.*

By knowing how much value we stand for and when it will accrue, we can propose our worth as an investment. We will know how good an option we are as a respository for our customers' discretionary funds. The higher our rate of return and the sooner it accrues, the better investment we will be. This is the "product" we will install in our customers' businesses, what we will put to work for them and what will improve their profits. When it is a good product, when its dollar-for-dollar performance is high, we can sell it with confidence and pride.

The value-basing of price forces us to know the value on which price will be based. Where can we look to find this value? It will always be in the life style or work style of our customers. We do not make value. Only our customers can make value. It comes out of the way they apply our products and services in their operations, their functions, their activities, and their processes. Value is performance value: value in use, not measurable at the point of manufacture or the point of sale but at the point of application and implementation.

Once we know a customer's added value from what we have sold to him, we have the reference point for learning what he is willing to pay for it. In brand language, once we can quantify the return we bring to a customer, he can determine the investment that appears fair to him for its acquisition. Here again, it is only our customers who can tell us. They and they alone possess the value. They and they alone, therefore, can estimate what it is worth to them.

In this, we are indeed fortunate. If we try to preempt the user's role in revealing our value to him along with its worth, we will be wrong far more often than we will be right. Even worse, we will probably be wrong on the low end in both assumptions. We will underestimate our value and, inevitably, what it is worth. As a result, we will leave money on the table from underpricing.

Underpricing is the vendor's irresistible temptation. Having no knowledge of what values he is contributing to his customers other than a "quality product" at a "competitive price," he remains unschooled in the impact he makes on customer businesses. The financial impact—how he is affecting customer profits—escapes him. By giving away his margins, he lowers customer cost. But could he improve customer profits even more at higher margins and, at the same time, improve his own profits? He will never know.

Brand Price Determination

Branding eliminates price negotiation. In the conventional sense, there is no price to negotiate. For a branded product or service, the traditional concept of price is replaced by investment. Brand price has a payback that exceeds it; therefore it cannot be treated as a cost. Its reference point becomes the return that the payback represents. That is its only point of comparison. Negotiating brand price is therefore a dialog about improving the relationship between the return and its investment. Can the return be increased without increasing the investment? Can the investment be reduced without diminishing the return?

A brand's equivalent of price negotiation centers on the three specifications of return on investment:

1. *How much?* What will the total return amount to, and can it be enlarged, either keeping the investment stable or even raising it?
2. *How soon?* When will the return start to flow, and when will all of it have accrued? Can it be accelerated?
3. *How sure?* What level of confidence can we have about how much and how soon, and how can we increase it without adding significantly to the investment?

Improvement in any one of them can significantly improve an investment's productivity.

The ideal return from investing in a brand is high in all three: a lot of profit accruing soon and with great certainty. This is an investor's nirvana. Rarely, if ever, can we meet all three specifications with the same investment. Incompatibilities are built into the returns from all investments. The greater the amount of return, the longer it may take to begin and totally accrue. It will also be less certain of full achievement. Smaller returns may accrue faster. They also have a greater level of confidence. In spite of their comparatively small size, they may have a greater impact on a customer because of the added time value of money they represent.

As a result of branding, a resolution of these forces will usually be made on the side of smaller, faster, and more certain returns. Large potential returns will be broken down into smaller successive bites so that the first installment can flow sooner and more surely. In this way, the brander offers early proof of his profitmaking performance. Furthermore, some of the initial profits he generates can be used in whole or in part to subsidize the customer's next investment. Growth, as a consequence, can become more self-funding.

Historically, for customers who buy it or buy based on it,

price is always a purchase that can be postponed. They want less price. They want it deferred as long as possible. They want to be carried. They want it to be surrounded by uncertainty because they hope to take advantage of any lack of commitment to a predetermined margin and use a supplier's cupidity as a lever to bend price backward. How different brand price is from vendor price negotiation. The promise of a return can never be postponed. Customers always want more, never less. They want it to flow as quickly as possible. And they want it made certain as close as possible to the 100 percent level of commitment.

For the brander, money talks. It speaks the customer's language of growth for his business, addresses the customer's bottom-line considerations, and focuses his attention on his imminent enrichment through new profits rather than on his progressive impoverishment through high prices. The brander puts negotiation on a positive plane, where it seeks greater earnings and becomes creative and expansionist, rather than essentially negative, as are the discussions of lower prices, free services, and competitive product liabilities that characterize vendor negotiations.

Rebranding

Brands outlive their branders. A brander has only one life, whereas a brand may have several commercial lifetimes, being born again as a brand after becoming mature. Through each rebirth, it can start a new S-curve and once again command the premium profits that accrue on its upside.

Rebranding should be a planned strategy. It should be readied in advance, because we can be sure that it will be required by all successful brands. Its application should come at the point where a brand's rate of growth has slowed and remained static for three consecutive quarters or has been negative for two quarters in a row. The longer the brander waits, the more difficult and less likely rebranding will be. Stasis or negative momentum will overtake the brand, competitors may outflank it, and markets may outgrow their perception of its value.

Branders must train themselves to think of maturity first. Otherwise, irreplaceable time will be lost, and irretrievable profits along with it, while the brand continues its descent into commodity status. Because the profits involved represent an opportunity cost and are therefore soft numbers, they generally go unquantified. But based on premium margins as they are, even in decline, lost profits are as unaffordable as they are unnecessary. Of all the ways in which managers leave money on the table, this is the most expensive.

The strategy for rebranding a brand in decline has three components: a reposition for the product, a redevelopment of its applications, and a reduction of its market.

Product Repositioning

A brand enters decline and becomes a candidate for rebranding when its value approaches its price. Since a brand's value is its true product, it must be repositioned so that it can again exceed its price when both are premium.

The positioning of a brand's value is dependent on the amount and type of impact it makes on customer businesses. This value may lose its premium worth due to an increasing competitive parity or a decreased customer dependence on the brander's applications capabilities. In their teaching role, branders grow customers intellectually as well as financially. As customers become smarter about the management of their own business functions, branders must stay one step ahead or lose their premium value.

Branders must ask what is happening to their financial impact. Why is it diminishing to the point that what was once premium value is approaching parity value? They must also ask what is necessary to redress the situation. Usually, there are two remedies:

1. The customer needs *greater* profits. His costs are increasing faster than the brander's ability to reduce them, or he has found that another brander can reduce them more.
2. The customer needs *faster* profits. His cash-flow requirements have increased because his investment program has accelerated or his sales are down.

The brander's reposition must answer his customers' needs. He must deliver greater profits or faster profits. Either the real value of the money he supplies or its time value will have to undergo change.

Applications Redevelopment

The brander's value is the direct result of his applications ability. He must always strive for the reputation of "best applier." This makes him dependent on two skills. One is his knowledge of the key cost and sales centers in customer businesses. The other is his expertise in improving their contributions to customer profits. His expertise will always be limited by his customer knowledge.

When the brander's margin of excess value over price dwindles in the perceptions of his market, the market may be telling him something. It may be saying that it is time to redevelop his applications ability. His learning curve may have stopped, allowing his competitors or his customers to catch up. Customer processes may have changed, shifting cost centers around and deemphasizing the negative contributions of traditional cost leaders such as labor, which is now running second to materials costs in manufacturing. Newer, more innovative applications may be needed to reduce costs below current levels where they have bottomed out, still unnecessarily high but stubbornly immune to the brander's skills. Or a customer's sales base may undergo alteration, replacing old markets with new ones.

If applications require redevelopment, it is either the fault of the brander's expertise (has it become obsolescent?) or his customer knowledge (has it become deficient?). The first fault is a sin against the brander. He has defaulted somewhere along the line in keeping up; his continuing self-education has been short-changed. The second fault is a sin against the brander's customers. He has defaulted in his penetration; his continuing customer education has short-circuited.

Market Reduction

Rebranding is a market-narrowing process. This is because broad, deep markets are costly. No matter how many customers a business serves, fewer than 20 percent will always account for as much as 80 percent of the profits. These are core customers, the heaviest profit contributors. As far as profits are concerned, they constitute "the market."

Mass markets can be a liability when a brand enters decline. The customers become too costly to identify, to convert, to serve, and to maintain. Most of them could be divested without serious loss. Those customers who cost more to serve than they return can be divested at a gain. By freeing resources from serving these low-profit contributors, the brander can concentrate his capabilities where the payoff is predictably greater: his core market.

Core customers are unique. They are the customers that the brander is actually growing the most. They work with the brander to implement his process-smarts into their operations so that their costs are minimized. They use the brander's market-smarts to help maximize their own shares of core markets that account for the majority of their own profits.

To rebrand, the brander must reduce his market to focus on his profit-based core. By comparison to his mass market, the core will appear small. But it is extremely powerful. Not only are these customers the most sizable source of profits; they also provide the highest quality profits because they are the most cost-effectively earned. The brander's revenue-to-investment and profit-to-revenue ratios are at their best when he does business with his core customers. They buy more. They take less time to buy. They repeat faster and they partner more closely.

Market reduction brings the brander back to what he is best at doing with the customers he is best at doing it with. For him, it represents a return to basics and, with it, a return to brand price, brand preference, and brand profits.

7
Partnering the Decision-Makers

Gaining Access to Customer Value-Adders
over the Life Cycle

No matter what business we are in, we have natural growth partners. They are other businesses whose growth is dependent in some significant way on our business. Identifying our growth partners is the most important act of managing our business.

If we know who our natural growth partners are and what they need from us in order to grow, we can dedicate our business to them from the outset. Our business will be a natural response to them. The organizational structure of our profit centers will represent a one-to-one relationship with the customer lines of business that we will grow. Our capabilities will be mirror-image responses to their needs. Our databases will contain knowledge of their growth problems and opportunities. Our business will be the reciprocal of our partners' businesses. For them, as for us, our dealings will be the ultimate in cost-effectiveness.

Identifying Growth Partners

If we manage a business that is a going concern, we have two types of natural growth partners. One type is businesses that are currently growing because of us, and the other is businesses that are growable by us but that we are not currently growing. If we are planning a startup business, all our growth partners will be in the second category. On the other hand, an up-and-running business automatically tells us who our growth partners are. We will already have discovered them—or, more likely, they will have discovered us, since we may have been selling them our products or processes while they were learning how to apply them to improve their profits. As a result, they are growing because of us. We can find them by segmenting the 20 percent or less of our customers that give us 80 percent or more of our profits. We profit from them because they know how to profit from us.

Customers that are already our greatest growth sources are also our greatest potential growth sources. Where there is currently much growth going on, there is prospectively more. This is so for several reasons. First, we are already growing each other, which suggests that our two businesses have a natural ability to grow each other even more. Second, we already know something about their business, and by using what we know as the foundation for knowing even more, we can grow them more. Third, we know some of their key decision-makers, and they can introduce us to others.

Customers we are currently growing are our corporate partners. Within each of their businesses, we will have to partner individually with two types of managers, both of whom will become our personal partners. One type will be their profit-center managers, the men and women who command the lines of business into which we sell. For them, we will have to add growth by increasing their profitable sales volume. The second type will be each customer's business-function managers, who supervise the operating functions we affect. We will have to reduce their negative contribution to growth by reducing the costs their operations throw off.

The businesses we are growing, along with the businesses we may be able to grow but have not yet converted to customers, are the keys to our growth. The very fact of their growth or potential for growth means they are eager consumers of cash. Their managers are heavy users of money to finance their growth. If we improve their profits, we can be important to them as a money source. Managers of growth businesses do not just need cash; they need it fast. They must direct it into the two functions of their business that control, or would otherwise constrain, their continued growth: production and sales. If we improve their profits, we can become one of their most important sources of fast cash flow.

Growth potential is the key partnering criterion. The growth potential of a customer partner determines our own. Only by growing can our partner make sure that our sales to him will turn over fast and *continue* to do so. This requires him to have high turnover in the sales he makes to his own customers. If they become stable, his turnover will stagnate. So will ours. For this reason stable customers—especially those with large shares of market that cannot be grown—are to be avoided. They may make good volume customers, but they are bad profit partners.

If we have a choice among growable customers, what fine-tuning criteria can we apply to discriminate among them? We should look for three attributes:

1. *Nascent opportunity.* We must seek the maximum opportunity to grow and be grown. Opportunity is the child of change. A growable customer that is undergoing reorganization or restructuring to provide further expansion is an enhanced partnership prospect. Change at the top of his management group is an added enhancement. Whenever major change is taking place, we have the chance to create new roles for ourselves, meet new or newly perceived needs in new ways, and form relationships with new managers who need to benefit immediately from our expertise.

2. *Positive attitude.* We must prefer to partner with cus-

tomers who prefer to partner. Their receptivity to our overtures will be greater that way, and so will their awareness and concern for their costs and revenues. We should expect them to be willing to share data with us and to contribute to our joint database. We should also expect them to create a growth team like ours to provide us with access to their decision-makers.

3. *High repute.* We must understand that the most sophisticated customers make the best partners. They will have the highest standards of performance. That will push us. They will have the most intelligent leaders in their industry. That will pull us. Our contribution to them will most likely be magnified: they will take what we give them and run with it. Our odds of success will increase, as will our ability to draw on references that will attract other sophisticated customers to us.

Income, impact, influence: a customer with whom mutual growth can be substantial, on whom we can make a major impact that will influence other growth customers to partner with us—these are our criteria. Instability in a customer business, especially management changes, may make a customer even more partnerable.

Choosing Growth Partners

Choosing growth partners is a two-step process. The first step is to pick out our natural partners: the customers we are growing right now, who are growing in whole or in part because of us. We can find them by seeking out the heaviest contributors to our profits; if they are growing us, it is a safe bet that we are growing them.

We should also identify other businesses that are growable by us but which we are not currently growing. This means that they have profitable sales opportunities we can help them exploit or business problems we can help them solve.

How can we know these things? How can we add even more growth to companies we are already growing, and how can we pinpoint the most profitable prospective customers for us to begin to grow?

Choosing Current Customers to Partner With

There are four questions we must answer about our current customers in order to determine which of them we should partner with:

1. *Who are we growing right now?* Some of our growth partners will be customers we are already growing, yet we may not be aware of our contribution to their growth. We may think we are merely selling to them. We think of them as our prime customers, our key accounts, or our heavy users. But they are actually "partners without portfolio." To determine if any one of them should be selected as our partner, we have to answer three more questions.

2. *How much are they growing us?* We may be unable to know the full extent to which we are bringing growth to a current customer. But we can much more easily calculate the sum total of profits by which we ourselves are growing as a result of doing business with him. There are four standards by which we should measure current customers: their absolute value to us, their comparative value to us ranked against our customer list as a whole, their contribution to our rate of growth, and the trend of their contribution to our growth rate over the past three years.

3. *How much more can we grow them?* Growth takes place in the future. Consequently, we must add a fifth standard to our calculations: what is the most likely projected rate of improved profits we can plan for in our growth of a customer's business over the next three years? If it is slowing steadily, becoming static, or declining, we may not have a true growth partner. Instead, we may have a mature customer to whom we

should continue to vend product performance values at competitive prices: a customer whom we should sell to and profit from, but with whom we will not grow.

4. *How much more can they grow us?* Because growth partnerships must be reciprocal, we must evaluate the most likely projected rate of our own profit growth over the next three years to see if it is increasing, becoming static, or declining as a result of each customer's contribution. If the projected incremental rates of growth are steadily increasing for both a customer and ourselves, we have a basis for growth partnering.

Choosing Prospective Partners

There are four questions to answer about prospective partners to determine which of them we should partner with:

1. *Who else can we grow?* Growable businesses that we are not currently growing are our source of market expansion. They may also be a source of diversification. To qualify as a growable customer a business must meet two criteria: its business problems must be susceptible to significant cost reduction by the application of our expertise, and our expertise must be able to increase significantly its profitable sales opportunities.

2. *How much will they grow us?* A business that is growable by us must be able to grow us in return. Our profit volume and its projected three-year rate of growth must meet or exceed our minimum threshold requirements, if we are to avoid opportunity loss.

3. *How can we grow them?* For each growable customer that we determine to be a potential partner, we must plan a growth strategy. The strategy will set forth the precise means by which we will add new profits to that customer's business. We will need to specify how much profit will accrue from reducing costs, how soon the profits will begin, and how long they will continue. We must also be able to calculate both the amount of profit from the new sales opportunities we will

make available and the markets they can be expected to come from.

4. *What capabilities must we invest in?* Growable customers that we are not currently growing may demand an extension of our existing capabilities. We may need to fortify our present strengths. We may also need to diversify by adding new strengths in such areas as research, product development, distribution, or sales strategies. By identifying our "growables" and matching their needs against our capabilities, we can answer the questions of whether or not we should diversify, what skills and systems we will need, and how much we will be required to invest in our growth.

Why Will Our Partners Grow Us?

Partnering requires two choices: our selection of the customers we will grow, and the customers' decision to partner with us. The customer will make this decision for three reasons:

1. *We are seen as an important source of growth profits.* The contribution of new assets that we can make to a customer must be significant. Only then will our partnership be important enough to both of us to merit top-level attention. To be an important source of growth means that we must account for worthwhile incremental profits on a customer's bottom line. We must also be able to deliver them in a timely fashion, recognizing the time value that money has for him. In this, we must be dependable. He must be able to count on us to improve his profits when we say we will and by the amounts we promise. Our importance to him will be in direct proportion to our reliability.

2. *We must be seen as one of the best investments in profit growth.* When a growth partner does business with us, he must perceive the price he pays to be an investment rather than a cost. The distinction is vital because only an investment yields a return. He must understand that what he is investing in is not our products or services or systems, not even our solutions. He is investing in new profits. The return he re-

ceives from his investment in us must be among the highest yields he can make.

Growth businesses need growers. They need as much growth as they can get as fast as they can get it. They fear the slowing of growth that will come from competitors or the obsolescence of their technological base by new developments. Every day of continued growth is worth its weight in gold. If our customer's growth rate stabilizes, he may never regain fast growth. We, in turn, may never regain him as a partner in our own growth.

Just how high does a customer's return on investing with us have to be? We must compare ourselves with the options. Normally a customer will invest in his own business in order to make profits. As his partner, we must offer him a better choice. We must make it more profitable for him to invest in our business. Either the investment he is required to make should be smaller for a similar return, or the return he receives from us should be larger, even though the investment may be correspondingly bigger.

3. *We must both have the same competitors.* When we sell products or services, positioning ourselves as one of a customer's alternate vendors, we are concerned only with defeating our own competitors—rival vendors. To be a partner means that we must concentrate on defeating our *customer's* competitors. Unless we have the same objective, we cannot be partners.

A customer's competitors are the constraints on his growth. He has two kinds. One is his current costs, against which he competes every day and which he must reduce if he is to improve his profits. Here, we must help him with our expertise. His second source of competition is sales opportunities. He competes for them every day, too, trying to win customers against his own rivals. If he is to improve his profits, he must increase his profitable penetration. Again we must help him with our expertise.

As our partners, our customers will grow us if we can make three transformations in our relationships with them.

First, we must transform ourselves from a supplier of

products and services to a supplier of profits. We must change ourselves from a manufacturing or service business into a financial service company whose product is profits.

Second, we must transform ourselves from representing an added cost to an added value. We must change our basis of doing business from selling performance values at a price to returning dollar values on an investment.

Third, we must transform our outlook, so that instead of competing against other companies in our own business, we compete against the cost and sales opportunity constraints of our partners. We must change our objectives to match those of our partners, so that we can defeat the same competitors. Once we do that, our partners will grow us for the same reasons, and in the same ways, that they grow themselves.

Partnering Through the Life Cycle

Each phase of the life cycle demands its own partnering strategy. From the very first words that we speak, customers must know that we know where they stand; that we recognize the multiple struggles of startup, the single-minded frenzy of growth, and the diminished options of maturity. At each phase of growth, the customer's objective is to put on weight; preferably it will be more muscle than fat. When maturity comes, a customer's objective switches to reducing. He will have to trim assets here, slim down participation in marginal markets there. Before we can play a helpful role, we must make it clear that we understand the problem.

When we approach a startup, we must try to help the customer's managers avoid the pitfalls and pratfalls that our experience tells us lie ahead, just beyond the range of their foresight. We can say, "Be careful. At startup, there is a natural tendency toward excessive staffing. Until your true labor requirements become known, you will probably feel more comfortable with too many people rather than what you think are too few. Yet you can saddle yourselves with tens of thousands of unnecessary dollars in costs that way. What if we can save that money for you at no risk that you will turn up short?"

A mature customer has no such problems, having solved his labor requirements long ago. So what do we say? "At maturity," we can say, "you learn that you have become the apex of a triangle. Customers converge on you from one side, competitors on the other. Both have the same objective: to squeeze your margins a little tighter. A perfectly natural reaction is to allocate an undue share of scarce resources to R&D to come up with something new that will justify a stronger margin. But this is not only expensive—it may not even work. What if we can help you raise margins on some of your current product lines instead, without having to renovate them?"

The following phase-by-phase analysis highlights partnering scenarios that we can use with customers wherever we may find them in their life cycles.

Partnering at Startup

A business at startup has one opportunity and four major problems. The opportunity is to make market entry and go commercial. Can we help? Can we underwrite entry for a customer business? Can we help him to make entry on plan, which means on time and within budget? Can we do even better: can we accelerate entry? By how much? Can we make it less costly? By how much? Even if we must make it more costly, can the customer's increased return from getting into business faster make up for it?

Four major problems stand between a customer's startup and entry.

1. *Who is our market?* Every startup business must find its market. It must beat the path to its market's door. The hard-core market of heavy profit contributors is never large. Nor does it necessarily announce itself. It must be sought out and captured. When a startup's managers are asked what drives the business, the startup's market must be the answer.

Can we help a startup customer develop his major markets? Can we make its market data-gathering less costly, more accurate or faster?

2. *How much product should we make?* A startup's initial investment in plant and equipment begins its physical asset base. Every asset imposes a cost. Every dollar of cost absorbs a startup's initial funding. It also soaks up profits once market entry has been achieved, delaying breakeven and the onset of positive cash flow.

Can we help a startup customer make optimal use of his investment in plant and equipment so that neither too little nor too much capacity results? Can we help make forecasting more accurate, driving the plant from the market? Can we help limit inventory, yet assure that distribution will be "just in time?"

3. *How can we assure maximum productivity?* Once a startup's overhead costs have been sunk into plant and equipment, the allocation of its working capital will determine how effectively its assets are being employed. Labor and materials are the principal operating costs of almost every manufacturing business. The dollar value of output produced by each unit of labor accounts for its productivity. The greater the number of product units produced by each unit of labor, the more productive it will be and the more cost-effectively will materials be utilized.

Can we help a startup customer achieve maximum productivity? Can we replace human labor's costs with a lower cost from automation? Can we increase materials productivity by improved forecasting and inventory control?

4. *How can we guarantee zero defects?* A startup's reputation depends on the quality of its first products. If they fail to perform as promised, the startup may be nipped in the bud. It may never recover from the embarrassment of failing in public. Warranty costs will consume profits from sales. Recall will dry up just-filled distribution pipelines. Even if lack of quality control is detected while products are still in the plant, scrap costs will rise, productivity will fall, and delivery dates will go unmet.

Can we help a startup customer improve his quality control? Can we help monitor production, measure adherence to specifications, or issue early warnings of going "off-spec" so that scrap rates can be reduced? Can we minimize downtime for repairs?

If we can create an initial market database or automate it, make forecasting more accurate and improve the mix of inventory, increase productivity, and help assure quality control, we can do business with a startup company. No matter what we sell, we can approach a startup's managers as the specialist in improving startup profit contribution.

Partnering at Entry

A customer business at entry has one opportunity and three major problems. The opportunity is to grow the business fast and become a big winner. Can we help? Can we compress a customer's entry and accelerate breakeven so that positive cash flow—the beginning of growth—can commence? By how much? Can we make entry less costly and growth more certain? By how much?

Three major problems stand between a customer's entry and growth.

1. *How can we get our first sales?* Making the initial sale is sometimes likened to getting the first olive out of the bottle. It rarely comes easy. The market, assuming there is one, must be mobilized. Negative cash flow continues. Work in process increases. Finished goods accumulate. The doubters and defeatists come out of the woodwork.

Can we accelerate an entry customer's first sale? Can we help to bring it in one month sooner; one week sooner; one day sooner? Can we help to identify the market? Can we help to train the sales force? Can we help to advertise, to create market awareness and positive attitude? Can we reduce a product's cost so that its price can be made more competitive?

2. *How quickly can we build share?* Once the first olive is out of the bottle, the second, third, and fourth olives become inventory. They too must be moved. The market of heavy, consistent customers—the repeat users who perceive pre-

mium value in a product and are willing to pay for it with a premium price—must be engaged. Market share must be built so that the dominant position of becoming the industry standard may be achieved. The race for growth is the race to amortize the costs invested in growth. It is also the race to get to market, and to dominate it, before competitors can intervene.

Can we accelerate a customer's successive sales? Can we help him reach the heavy profit-contributing core of the market? Can we educate, motivate, or help find stimulating ways to compensate the sales force? Can we play the role of turnover specialist?

3. *How can we maintain reliability?* Product returns, repairs, and recall are the enemies of market entry. They can ruin reputation, deplete distribution channels of stock, and suffocate an emerging business in its crib. Driven by the pressure to fill the pipelines and start cash flow, a company can experience severe stress in manufacturing and quality control. Systems that looked good on paper, or on pilot runs during startup, may break down.

Can we help maintain an entry customer's supply of marketable products? Can we minimize defects or detect them before they go out the door? Can we monitor and measure his vital processes to keep them on time and on plan?

Partnering in Growth

A customer business in growth has one major opportunity, two of the same three major problems it had at entry, and two new problems. The opportunity is to maintain a high and increasing rate of growth quarter after quarter, year after year. This will define the business as a growth business. Can we help? Can we help the customer earn consistently high margins and multiply their value by expanding sales volume so that growth profits continue to accumulate at a rising rate? Can we play the role of turnover specialist for our customers?

Growth businesses carry over with them the two entry

problems of building market share quickly and maintaining product reliability along with productivity. Failure in either area can terminate the growth phase.

In growth, there are two other problems that stand between early profitmaking and its perpetuation into continued earnings.

1. *How can we become self-financing?* A growth business has two obligations. One is to become self-financing so it can pay its own way, free from being a consumer of corporate funds. The other is to become a supplier of funds to the corporate treasury so that the company's slow-growth or no-growth businesses can be supported and so that new startups can be capitalized. Self-financing must come first. Cash flow becomes the essence of growth business life.

Can we accelerate a growth customer's cash flow? Can we help billings go out faster? Can we help receivables come in faster? Can we maximize the realization on each receivable that is collected? Can we help allocate his resources so that cash goes for investments that are productive of more growth rather than nonproductive or counterproductive? Can we help reduce costs so that more of the cash that comes in can flow to the bottom line?

2. *What do we do for an encore?* A successful growth business develops a market franchise—in effect, a license issued by its market to help the market grow. Once awarded, a franchise offers room for expansion. Our customer's market asks our customer, How else can you grow us? There is another question for us. Every growth business contains the seeds of its maturity. When maturity takes over, growth profits first slow down and then taper off to low commodity levels. Another growth business will be needed to take its place as a big winner. The time to start a new S-curve is always while an existing growth business is still growing so that there is never a valley of depressed earnings in between the peaks.

Can we help plan, organize, or otherwise contribute to a new startup business for our growth customer? Can we conceptualize, test, or help manufacture or market a new product extension for the existing business? Can we bring another growth business together with our customer's business so that similar capabilities can be reinforced by sharing or exchanged without investing?

Partnering at Maturity

A customer business at maturity has one major opportunity and two major problems. The opportunity is to increase the return from its asset base, all of which has been expensively bought and paid for. Failing that, its sole recourse is to minimize the base. Can we help increase a customer's sales volume at existing margins? Can we help reduce costs so that existing margins can be preserved, yet price can be lowered?

Two major problems stand between the continuation of a customer's mature business and its demise by writeoff or divestiture.

1. *How can productivity be improved?* Because the products of mature businesses are commodities, they are price-sensitive. Their low margins, the results of their loss of competitive differentiation, must be made up by volume. But volume adds cost to an already expensive asset base. The only way to afford the added cost of volume is to reduce unit cost. This means that as many units of marketable product as possible must be manufactured and sold for each dollar they cost. The more units of product made per dollar and the more units of product sold per dollar, the greater the productivity.

Can we help increase a mature customer's volume while decreasing his unit cost? Can we help maintain production, reducing downtime and scrap? Can we help reduce the cost content of other operations by eliminating some of their component parts, combining them, or automating them? Can we make buying cheaper than making, or can we find ways by which making is cheaper then buying?

2. *How can sales be improved?* The demand for cash is insatiable at maturity. There is no such thing as enough sales or enough market share. Forces are always working against

expanding sales. Competition is one. Competitors fight to capture shares of the customer's market. Technology is another counterforce. It makes a customer's existing performance capability obsolete. The market itself is a third force. It constantly increases its pressure for more product performance at lower price. This causes our customers to make renewed investments in technology, yet deprives their mature businesses of the earnings necessary to finance them or recover their costs.

Can we help expand a mature customer's market, bringing new customers to him? Can we help expand his share of the current market, increasing average order size? Can we help increase his margins even though his market, or his market share, is decreasing?

The Resolution of Comfort and Urgency

No matter what phase of a customer's life cycle we choose for our penetration, the preconditions for partnering will be the same.

The universal precondition for partnering is the customer's perception that a supplier represents a source of added profit value. This is the minimum requirement for a partner. Otherwise, who needs him? Unless a candidate for partnering brings significant new funds to a customer, all he will be able to offer is an added cost. Bearers of added costs are never partners. They are vendors, and the challenge they present to a customer is to make costs reducible.

If we simply propose the added value of new profits that we can supply, however, we may be able to penetrate but we will not necessarily be a partner. We become a partner only when two further conditions are met. The customer's *comfort* needs must be fulfilled. At the same time, he must be moved by a sense of *urgency* to act now. These conditions appear to be paradoxical. Comfort requires time, usually more than urgency will permit. Urgency requires commitment, usually in

advance of comfort. How can we reconcile these two contra-
dictory needs? In order to penetrate as a partner, *we must make
urgency comfortable.*

Making Partnering Comfortable

The interaction of comfort and urgency is based on the
three specifications of profit improvement: how much, how
soon, and how sure. Comfort comes from being sure. For a
customer to be sure that partnering with us is a good idea—
that it is valuable to take us into his business as a co-
contributor of earnings—we must satisfy him about two
things:

1. We know his business, specifically the dollar values of
   the cost problems and sales opportunities in the operations that we can affect.
2. We know our business, specifically the dollar values of
   the solutions we can implement in his operations and
   the most cost-effective ways to achieve them.

We cannot talk our way to satisfaction. We must prove it.
This is the partial role of our cost-benefit analysis, which doc-
uments our knowledge of the customer's current costs and opportunities and which appears side by side with our proposal
to improve their contributions to his profits. But it is actually
our proposal telling the customer how we are going to get
from where he *is now* to where he *will be as a result of our
partnership* that is the key to his comfort. Our solution must
make sense as well as dollars.

The burden of comforting the customer, therefore, rests
with our solution: the package of people, products, services,
training, and financing that will be integrated into the customer's operations to effect change. Of these, the single most
important component is our people—the consultative appliers, installers, and implementers, whose expertise and experience are the crucial ingredients in making our products,

services, and systems perform as profit contributors inside a customer's business.

Our products must work. Our services must help our products work. Our systems must be comprehensive and integrated so that everything works together. But it is our people who prescribe their optimal mix and who put them to work, train the customer's people to work them, monitor their work, calculate the values they add, and seek to upgrade them. It is our people with whom a customer's people will partner. There is no substitute for the most partnerable people. If all we have to offer is the most performance in our products, all we will be able to penetrate will be the customer's purchasing level.

Making Partnering Urgent

Customers derive their comfort from our people. But they derive urgency from somewhere else: from how much added profit we propose to them, how soon that profit will begin to flow onto the customer's balance sheet, and how much delay will cost.

Urgency is dollar-derived. The dollars must be significant, both in sum and as a return on the customer's investment. Because dollar value has a time value, the customer's return on his investment must start its flow as soon as possible. In many cases, this quick start is even more important than richness of return. This is true for all cash-hungry businesses, such as new entries and customer businesses in their growth phases, whose need to feed the sales cycle is paramount.

The first moment when new profits will be delivered is one of the two factors that generate urgency. The sooner they can be delivered, the better. Early profits are always more desirable than later ones. They are also more valuable and more believable. Profits too long postponed become ephemeral, losing credibility in direct proportion to their postponement. Since they are so far off in the future, there is no apparent urgency in committing to them. What difference will one more day make?

The second generator of urgency is the dollar difference that will be made by each day of deliberation, debate, and delay. Here, we must prove two things. One is obvious—each day's delay postpones the onset of profits by at least that day's worth of time. Profits that could be available will not be. This will incur an opportunity cost, the loss that the customer will suffer from a missed opportunity. This is the second proof we must document. It will be a different number than the dollar value of each day's delay. Opportunity cost will always be greater, since it must include not only the per diem dollar value of lost profits but the potential invested value of those dollars—how much the customer could have added to his profits by reinvesting them in his business or somewhere else, even at simple bank interest.

Building partnerable teams is our responsibility. They are the comfort-bringers of our penetration strategy. They must seek out responsible partners on the customer side who respect the time value of money and who understand, and will not tolerate, opportunity loss. They will supply the urgency in our relationships. Unlike vendors, who often create artificial urgency to "buy now," we must evoke urgency in our customers based on the added values of new profits that, together, we can create now. If we make customers comfortable about our partnerability, it will be they—not we—who will translate their urgency into our penetration.

8
Pairing Off the Partners

Linking Life Cycles for Maximum Matching

Any life-cycle phase of a customer business can be penetrated if we can partner our objectives with the top priorities of the customer's business managers. They know what they have to do in order to achieve their profit goals, what costs they must avoid or reduce, which operations must be made more productive, and which markets must yield increased revenues and earnings. Our job is to add incremental value to these goals.

Life-cycle penetration opportunities are remarkably constant. We can depend on them. Phase by phase, they are always predictable. Based on the position of our own business on the life-cycle curve, some customers will be easier for us to penetrate than others. This will be due to the harmonies and disharmonies—the similarities and differences—that are created by the relative positions of our two businesses.

If we and a customer are both entrepreneurial businesses, in our entry phases or growing, we will generally find that likes attract. The same will be true if we are both mature. Opposites may be made attractive too, if we understand the inherent assets and liabilities of an entrepreneur and a mature business working as partners. While generalizations like growth and maturity are managerial, organizational, and operational in their impacts, they are psychological truths as well. In this regard, our challenge is to understand the needs of maturity even though we ourselves may be entrepreneurial—and, conversely, to understand the needs of an entrepreneurial business if we are mature.

If we are at the entrepreneurial stage of our business, mature customers can give us legitimacy and provide a reliable, repetitive, and reputable platform for our growth. By the same token, as an entrepreneurial supplier we can revivify a mature customer. Two entrepreneur businesses have the potential to augment each other's growth profits. A similar potential exists for two mature businesses, although there is the hidden peril that they will both leave huge sums of money on the table because of the ritualistic manner (like elephants mating) in which they practice penetration.

Figure 8-1 shows the options for pairing off. Boxes 1 and 2 of the matrix represent the opportunity for high growth at high risk. Boxes 3 and 4 are the converse, offering growth and risk that are both low. Integrating boxes 1 and 4 or boxes 2 and 3 generates unpredictability, with a promise of significant advantages to both partners.

Pairing Off with an Entrepreneur Customer

To maximize his penetration opportunity, a supplier must qualify an entrepreneur customer's needs in one of three ways:

1. The customer needs new profits as fast as possible. How soon can he receive them from the supplier?
2. The customer needs new profits as often as possible. How can he keep getting them from the supplier?
3. The customer needs new profits as reliably as possible. How much can he depend on the supplier?

These three qualifications—how soon, for how long, and how sure—are the critical factors in incremental profitmaking

Figure 8-1. **Supplier-customer life-cycle matrix.**

High Growth–High Risk

1	2
Growth Supplier	Growth Customer
3	**4**
Mature Supplier	Mature Customer

Low Growth–Low Risk

for an entrepreneur customer. They are the objectives that we will have to meet if we want to pair off.

Penetration Potential of an Entrepreneur Supplier

Entrepreneurial businesses in their entry and growth stages have a natural affinity for one another. They have similar objectives—each wants to grow. They are operating under similar time pressures—each needs to grow fast. They have similarly flat management hierarchies—decision-makers and deal-makers are often one and the same, so they can reach agreements quickly and take decisive action on them then and there. Whether selling or buying, each business knows the time value of money and the penultimate value of cash flow at the early stage of the life cycle. And because both management teams are entrepreneurial, their styles of doing business, their tempos, and their frontier-type organization cultures can mesh well.

An entrepreneurial supplier is likely to be a source of leading-edge technology and of innovative products and systems that have been commercialized from it. They may help a startup customer gain competitive sales faster and, if he can prove the value of his differentiation to his own customers, earn premium margins. Because of this opportunity to make money by making a splash as the newcomer to a market, an entrepreneur customer may be more penetrable than a mature customer by an entrepreneur supplier.

Penetration Potential of a Mature Supplier

A mature business has a lot to offer an entrepreneurial growth customer. In order to penetrate so that it can become a major source of supply, the mature business will have to avoid a clash of cultures.

The two businesses may have dissimilar objectives—one will want to grow and the other may want to retain its stability or turn around a decline. They may have dissimilar time pressures—one needs to grow fast and the other may prefer slower, but sure, growth. They will probably have dissimilar management hierarchies—decision-makers and deal-makers will be one and the same for the customer but can be several, and several layers removed, for the supplier. Cash flow will be vital for the customer, while margins (earnings from sales rather than sales themselves) may be dominant for the mature supplier. His marketing strategy may be based on customer cost reduction, a much lower priority for a growth customer than sales development. The two management teams will have different styles of doing business, different tempos, and different cultures.

Yet a mature supplier possesses vast knowledge of his product or service and its application. He may be the owner of the industry norms for the customer operations he can affect. He is likely to stockpile cadres of applications specialists, training specialists, financial specialists, and other expert resource people who can complement the customer's staff. He may have reams of historical data on customer markets and competitors, information that no growth supplier could have yet accessed. His penetration potential will depend in general on how well he can apply his assets to the customer's action-driven style and his specific needs for sales growth.

Pairing Off with a Mature Customer

To maximize his penetration opportunity, a supplier must qualify a mature customer's needs in two ways:

1. The customer needs as much new profit as possible. How much can he obtain from the supplier?
2. The customer needs new profits as reliably as possible. How much can he depend on the supplier for them?

"How much" and "how sure" are the critical factors in incremental profitmaking for a mature customer. They are the objectives that we will have to meet if we want to pair off.

Penetration Potential of an Entrepreneur Supplier

An entrepreneur business in its entry and growth stages has a lot to offer a mature customer. In order to penetrate so that it can become a major source of supply, the entrepreneur business will have to avoid the same clash of cultures that can prevail when a mature supplier tries to penetrate an entrepreneur customer. In terms of objectives, time pressures, marketing strategies, and styles of doing business, there are far more differences between them than similarities.

An entrepreneur supplier may appear pushy and overly aggressive in sales style. To the supplier, the mature customer may appear to take forever to make decisions, shield its multilayered decision-making hierarchy from the supplier so that joint planning is denied, make eventual decisions more for political reasons than for their technological or financial impact, and place competitive price at the pivotal point of its purchases.

A mature customer will tend to look at a supplier's track record rather than at his breakthrough technology, preferring to be the supplier's second customer rather than his guinea pig. The more futuristic the supplier's technology, the greater will be the customer's reluctance to incur the risk of failure by being first. Yet there are always mature customers who realize that an entrepreneur supplier's successful track record can begin with them and that being first can afford a unique opportunity to turn maturity back to growth.

Penetration Potential of a Mature Supplier

Just as with two entrepreneurs doing business, two mature businesses have a natural affinity. They have compatible styles, cultures, and senses of time. Each can make the other feel comfortable. Often, their value systems are virtually interchangeable. So are their managers.

In mature supplier-customer relationships, the ultimate downside risk is that costs will be exchanged instead of profits being mutually improved. The supplier transfers his costs to the customer. If there is a margin, it will be slim. The customer transfers to the supplier as much as possible of the costs of processing proposals, holding inventory, training his people in the supplier's methods, maintaining the supplier's system, and even financing it. When all is said and done, each may break even on his transactions. Cash flow, not profits, maintains the pairing.

No matter who is doing the penetrating, entrepreneur or mature supplier, mature customers are difficult to penetrate. Two types of opportunity hold out the greatest promise for penetration. One is the startup business ventures within an otherwise mature customer. This type of business can be penetrated as if it were entrepreneurial. The second type is the mature business that wants to turn back to growth or that needs to improve its image for divestiture. This type of business can also be penetrated as if it were entrepreneurial.

Where does that leave the bulk of mature customer businesses, the stale ones whose commodity products and services inch along year by year for only incremental gains in profits? They are perennial customers for cost reduction. Suppliers at any stage of their life cycle who are experts in cost control, and who can prove it, always have something to offer and can penetrate at will. The hard-won margins they will receive in return, however, may make this kind of business little more than incremental to the supplier's penetration objectives.

Growing Old Together

One of the most debilitating business practices is the tendency of a supplier and his customer to grow old together. This does not require them to have a long, continuing relationship. It means that, wittingly or otherwise, each is aiding and abetting the other's maturity. Two mature businesses enter their business relationship already predisposed to work with each other in ways that are comfortable, and therefore conservative and traditional, for them. Left to their own devices, each will reinforce their mutual propensities to embrace certainty, avoid risk, and constrain costs.

The customer will worry more about what he pays out than what he brings in. The supplier will worry more about what he charges than the value he can add. The tried and true, their shared experience about "what works," will be the basic platform for the relationship. Innovation will come hard because its sponsors will be few, its opportunities rare, and its chances for acceptance slim.

Mature companies settle down with each other quickly. Their top people share a common frame of reference. They both know the same set of rules and that makes it easy to do business together; neither is building a learning curve at the other's expense. Each "does right" by the other. When there is abrasion, it is almost always in the area of price. The supplier comes to dread announcing price increases as much as his customer is distressed to hear about them.

What they should dread, of course, is the standardization of sameness in their relationship. The supplier puts little or no pressure on the customer to innovate. If he does, the process for suggesting radical change has itself become so routine, and its conclusion so predictable, that it becomes a mere pro forma gesture. On the other hand, the customer puts little innovative pressure on the supplier. He imposes quality standards that, while they may change in degree, are conceptually familiar. Additional free services may be requested to atone for price increases. Inventory policy, and therefore delivery schedules, may be altered from "just in case" to "just in time." But these things do not represent innovation. Neither business is threatened by becoming significantly more valuable.

Because threat is typically absent, mature relationships are noted for longevity. They are also notable for huge opportunity loss, which is calculable but rarely calculated. Because the supplier sees only harm in rocking the boat, and because the customer's vested interests seek to protect their investments, opportunities go by the boards. New concepts await trial and verdict elsewhere. If they are attended at all, it is to see them prove themselves over and over elsewhere rather than to reach out and grasp their leading edge. Arrogance that "we must be doing something right" creeps in on both sides. Often it is compounded by ignorance of other options that, if they were known, would be treated with aversion.

Growing old together almost always ends catastrophically. When the customer finally declines, downsizing his business commitments, suppliers who survive the cut will have to downsize too. If the customer's management undergoes change and the old managers go, many of their favored supplier relationships will go with them. Sometimes the calamity is a different kind. An innovative supplier breaks through the customer's defenses, perhaps by migrating from a related area of the business as a whole or coached by a fan inside the customer's management hierarchy who fears a continuation of the past more than the chanciness of the future. When that happens, the old supplier becomes preempted overnight. He will be asked, Why didn't you ever come to us with something like this? At that point, it will do little good to say that it would probably have been to no avail.

Niching into Countercyclical Business

Countercyclical relationships, where there appears to be little or no compatible linkage, can nonetheless be achieved by niching a new opportunity rather than confronting an established supplier head-on. By outflanking a competitor, the lack of life-cycle similarity can be positioned as an advantage over him as long as the customer can be made aware, or already understands, that an atypical problem or opportunity prevails.

Niching is a successful countercyclical strategy for two kinds of penetration situations. One is a mature customer innovating a new product or new business. This may permit a mature supplier to be circumvented by an entrepreneur. The other situation occurs when a growth customer has a business that has become mature, either because its technology has been neutralized by competition or its market has itself matured. This may permit a mature supplier to circumvent an entrepreneur.

Opportunities for niching occur as the byproducts of change. Something new is taking place in a customer's business while everything else remains the same. It may be growth that is new. Or it may be maturity. The customer is challenged to adapt to it. He may be inexperienced. If his business is mature, it may have been a long time between growth businesses. Who can help? If his business has known only a high rate of growth and then suddenly slows, he may have no experience in dealing with the change. Or it may not attract his interest, especially if he has a new growth business to launch. Who can help? If the suppliers who are already in place cannot claim sufficient expertise and experience that is equal to but opposite from their linked compatibility, they may be supplanted.

In this type of situation, countercyclical positioning can be an asset. But it can be marketed only if its value to the customer is shown to exceed competitive values from the supplier who is already in place. This means that his values must be quantified in dollar terms so that the customer can measure the worth of a countercyclical partnership.

Customers measure the value of trading away cyclical compatibility in one of two ways. If a customer cost center is involved—such as the manufacturing operation of a new product line—the value of a countercyclical supplier will be calculated as costs avoided, reduced, or deferred. Scrap costs may be reduced. Downtime costs may be avoided. Startup costs may be eliminated for some operations. A mature supplier may have superior skills in these areas from his work with similar operations over the years, both in customer organizations and within his own business. When it comes to cost control, no one may have a better or longer track record, which even an entrepreneur customer will recognize.

In the case of customer profit centers, an entrepreneur supplier may have a countercyclical opportunity to penetrate a mature customer if the entrepreneur's process or product confers a sales advantage. This will be especially desirable if the mature customer has developed a new business or needs to make one of his mainstream businesses recompetitive. Sales revenue improvement, not cost reduction, will be the tradeoff value. The amount of the new value and how quickly it can be brought on stream will determine the availability of the niche.

You Are What You Link

Businesses become known by the customers they link to. Entrepreneur businesses that link to other entrepreneur businesses become known as hotshots. They act as multipliers of growth, accelerating already volatile S-curves of growth businesses to make them go higher even faster. When entrepreneur businesses link with mature customers, they can exert a recompetitive impact on a dormant business that revivifies its sales and profits and renews its market position.

Mature businesses that link to each other become known as transferers of technology and costs. Many have a stimulating effect by injecting their sciences into a customer, such as automating his office or factory systems or renovating a process in his plant operations. Inevitably, they trade costs: the customer trades the cost of purchase for the supplier's costs of research and development, manufacturing, and marketing. Very often this kind of trade breaks even. Neither partner's profit is significantly improved.

Every business becomes what its linkages says it is, no more and no less. A company that links to developing sales of growth businesses, whether they are freestanding or occur as ventures in mature companies, is a growth business. A company that links to cost-centered situations, such as reducing the investment base of mature businesses or even avoiding costs in emergent businesses, is going to have at least mature overtones, and may be wholly characterized by them. If it deals primarily with mature customers, its own maturity will be a foregone conclusion.

The choice of linkages is therefore crucial to the position of a business in its industry. As the old adage says, a business will be known by the positions of the customers it keeps. Businesses in good fiscal health maintain themselves in a growth mode. They are periodically growing new profit curves and attending to the rate of growth of their base businesses. They do this by seeking out growth partners, businesses that they can grow. They link their growth to the growth of their partners, driving their profits from their customers' increased revenues and decreased costs. The 20 percent or so of the businesses they depend on for the 80 percent of their profits are all at growth points in their life cycles, either as new grown or regrown customers. Because they are linked to them by their penetration, they are in the same growth position.

9

Overcoming the Vulnerabilities

Invigorating the Customer's Life Cycle

To the vendor with something to sell, whose competitive performance will determine his price, the customer often appears impregnable. Multitudes of suppliers bid for the customer's business. All meet his specifications. In ever-decreasing numbers, they pass through his successive cuts until, finally, he chooses one or two finalists. They may not make much money on the deal, but they will have the business. At times, this may be their only differentiation.

The winners will ask, How could we have penetrated faster, cheaper, higher, and come away with a better price? The losers will have a question of their own: How could we have penetrated? As a general rule, neither will find the answer. Each will go on doing what all vendors do best—putting a price on performance and being prepared to deal and discount their margins away.

The answers are unlikely to be found because they do not lie with the suppliers. They lie with the customer. The customer knows how to penetrate his business. He knows where the windows are, what the priorities are for entering them, and how much it may be worth to him to have some of them filled. He knows these things because he looks at his business from a perspective that his vendors never see. The customer sees his business from the inside. Vendors see it from without. Outside, it appears impenetrable. The customer, however, knows only too well where his vulnerabilities are.

Some of a customer's vulnerabilities come from his own misdoings. He miscalculates or mismanages. But this happens infrequently, in the manner of an Edsel or PCjr or New Coke, and when it does, its effect is blown out of proportion to its number or frequency. Most of a customer's vulnerabilities are thrust upon him, just as his opportunities are, by the position of his business in its life cycle.

The customer sees these aspects of his business, which constitute the great majority of his cost problems and sales opportunities, close up. His vendors, if only they will look, can see them equally well from the outside. They are visible to both parties because they can be predicted by both.

A customer sees the opportunities of a startup business to grow into a big winner. He also sees its vulnerability to premature decline—because of products that are out of specification, inventory that is out of stock, or a sales strategy that is out of gear with its market segment. A vendor can see these problems, too. They are inherent with startup businesses. But he may fail to focus on them because his product is the apple of his eye.

A customer sees the opportunities of turning around a mature business, restructuring it to make it recompetitive. He also sees the potential for killing the goose that lays the golden eggs. He knows he might cut into muscle instead of just cutting out fat, antagonize distribution instead of clearing out the channels, or leave traditional customers uncovered instead of consolidating all sales through a single contact. A vendor can see these problems, too. They are inherent with mature businesses. But he may fail to focus on them because his product is still the apple of his eye.

The problems and opportunities that accompany each stage of a customer's life cycle—indeed, that define the life-cycle stage and can therefore be predicted for it—are visible, tangible, and amenable to action by customers and their vendors alike. They are the only attributes of customer businesses about which this is true. Much else about someone else's business, like one's own, will always remain obscure. But one thing is incontestible: If we know what phase of the life cycle a customer's business is in, we can tell him his risks and rewards; his costs and benefits; his problems and opportunities.

If we can *tell him the solutions* for his problems—profits to replace direct costs—and ways to seize his opportunities—profits to replace opportunity costs—we can penetrate his business.

Appendix A
The Evaluation Process for Calculating Incremental Profit

Customer businesses have a single overriding objective: to improve their profits on a progressive, continuous basis. They are evaluated by outsiders—just as they evaluate themselves—on the amount of their profit growth and its rate. Customer profit improvement begins at this point where they know the current profits that you are going to improve: how they make their money right now. This is the starting point.

Knowledge of how customers make profit starts with their own records of performance. For public companies, these are the balance sheet and the income statement that appear in their annual reports and 10 K publications. Privately held companies must be assessed by speculation, with the best clues obtained from comparison with public companies in the same industry.

Proposal Background
from the Customer's Balance Sheet

A balance sheet is a snapshot of a business that shows its financial condition at the moment it is snapped. If you learn how to read it, you can picture the financial structure of a customer's business, and this will be very useful in helping you spot your best opportunities for profit improvement.

Balance sheets can take many forms, and the items that appear on them may vary according to the character of each business and its particular circumstances. A conventional balance sheet appears in Figure A-1.

To understand the character of the underlying funds, you must translate the customer balance sheet into the form shown in Figure A-2. In effect, A-2 is an X-ray of A-1.

The left-hand side of Figure A-2 represents the funds invested in the business operations of a customer. It shows at a

Figure A-1. **Balance sheet expressed as a statement of assets and liabilities.**

BALANCE SHEET	
Assets	Liabilities
Current assets	Current liabilities
	Long-term liabilities
Fixed assets	Capital (capital stock and retained earnings)

particular point in time where and in what form these funds reside. Current assets are the funds invested in the circulating capital of the business. Funds invested in the facilities used to operate the business are fixed assets.

The right-hand side of Figure A-2 shows the current sources of the funds that have been invested. From it, we can determine the specific proportion of the customer's total invested funds that has been contributed by vendors, banks, bondholders, and by the owners. When the dollar values assigned to the items on each side are totaled, a balance sheet must balance.

As a rule, management of the left-hand side of the balance sheet, representing the funds invested in a customer's operations, is the responsibility of operating management. The

Figure A-2. **Balance sheet expressed as a statement of funds invested and sources of funds.**

BALANCE SHEET	
Funds Invested	Sources of Funds
Circulating capital	Vendors Banks (short-term)
	Banks Insurance Companies Bondholders (long-term)
Facilities	Stockholders

right-hand side of the balance sheet, representing the sources of funds, is the responsibility of financial management. Since the cost of acquiring and maintaining funds differs depending on their source, money management is an important function contributing to profitability.

Proposal Background from the Customer's Income Statement

Increases or decreases in the value of a customer company's capital are generally the result of one or more of three conditions:

1. Capital value will increase if additional capital is obtained.
2. Capital value will decrease if dividends are paid out.
3. Capital value will increase if the net result of operations is a profit and will decrease if the net result of operations is a loss.

By far the most significant factor in determining capital value is the net result of operations or the earning power of the business. This aspect of profitmaking is reported in a separate document known as the income statement or profit and loss (P&L) statement. On it, profit appears as the remainder of revenues after expenses have been subtracted. This statement of profit on the bottom line is the benchmark from which your profit improvement objectives must take off. How much better can you do than the customer is already doing? Every dollar you can add represents incremental gain for the customer and provides the basis of incremental price for you.

The P&L statement also shows you where a customer's money goes—where investment is most intensive and where any reduction will be welcome. A typical dealership or distributor will state its intensiveness like this:

	($000)
Materials	850
Labor	1,500
Overhead	900

You may not be able to reduce fixed assets, at least not in the short term. But labor and materials costs are prime targets for cost-reduction proposals.

The Circulating Capital Principle

Profit is made by the circulation of business capital. Every business is founded on capital, or funds that start in the form of cash. The objective of business is to make that initial cash grow into more cash. This is accomplished by circulating the capital, the initial cash, through three transfer points, each of which adds value:

1. The initial cash circulates first into *inventories*.
2. Then the inventories circulate into *receivables*.
3. The receivables finally circulate back into *cash,* completing one cycle.

This three-step process demonstrates the principle of circulating capital. Every business depends on it for its income.

Circulating capital is the current assets of a business. They go to work in profitmaking as soon as cash is invested in accumulating inventories. Every time raw materials are purchased or processed, inventories come into existence. Another name for production scheduling could really be inventory conversion. Manufacturing adds further to the values of inventories, and so do all the other processing functions of a business that transfer value from cash to product costs on a dollar-for-dollar basis.

Figure A-3 shows the profitmaking process that occurs as capital funds circulate through a customer's business. At A the funds are in the form of cash. As the business operates, the

Figure A-3. Profitmaking through capital circulation.

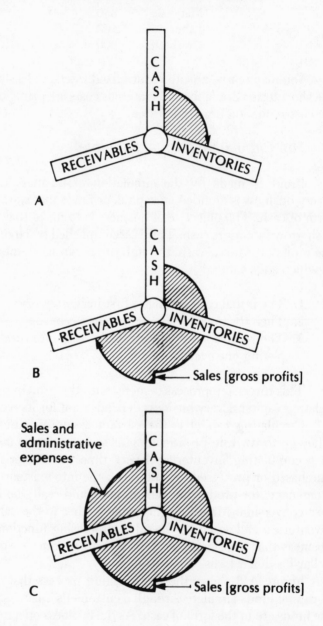

funds change form. The initial cash is transferred into inventories, as raw materials are purchased, labor is paid, and finished goods are manufactured and sometimes transported from plant to warehouse.

When sales occur at B, funds flow from inventories—the manufactured goods—into receivables. As they flow, the magnitude of the funds increases since inventories are valued at cost and receivables are valued at selling price. This increase represents the gross profit on sales. The greater the gross profit rate, the greater the increase in funds during each rotation of the capital circulation cycle.

At C, the funds earned by the collection of receivables flow back once again into cash. Before they do, they are reduced by the sales and administrative expenses that have been disbursed throughout the operating cycle.

At this point, one full cycle of capital circulation has been completed. It has resulted in an increase in the number of dollars in the circulating capital fund. This increase is the difference between gross profits and selling and administration expenses. In other words, a profit is made when the circulating capital of the business turns over one cycle. The more cycles through which you can help turn your customer's circulating capital during an operating year, the greater the profit the customer can earn. This is the principle of *turnover.*

The Turnover Principle

The circulation of capital funds in a customer's business takes on meaning only when it relates to time. Since capital funds turn over in a complete cycle from cash to inventories, then to receivables, and finally back into cash again, their rate of flow can be measured as the rate of turnover. The faster the turnover, the greater the profit.

Stepping up a customer's turnover rate through profit improvement is the consultative sales representative's most important function. Unless your profit projects are by and large directed to improving the turnover of the capital employed in your customer's business—especially the capital that is in the form of inventories—you cannot accomplish your mission.

Turnover will generally offer more opportunities than any other strategy for profit improvement. The most common way to improve turnover rate is through increased sales volume and lowered operating fund requirements. In some situations, turnover may be improved by decreasing sales or even increasing the investment in operating assets.

You are in an excellent position to help improve a customer's turn of circulating capital since, as Figure A-4 shows, the drive wheel that rotates capital is sales. You must continually search for the optimal relationship between your customer's sales volume and the investment in operating funds required to achieve it. At the point where the optimal relationship exists, the turnover rate will yield the best profit.

In Figure A-4, the circumference of the sales wheel represents $200,000 worth of sales during a 12-month operating period. The sales wheel drives a smaller wheel representing circulating capital. The circumference of the smaller wheel equals the amount of dollars invested in working funds, in this case $100,000. Enclosing the circulating capital wheel is a larger wheel, also driven by sales, that represents the total capital employed. It includes the circulating capital of $100,000 plus another $100,000 invested in plant and facilities. Thus the circumference of the wheel representing total capital employed is $200,000, equal to the sales drive wheel.

When annual sales are $200,000 and total capital employed in the operation is $200,000, the annual turnover rate of total funds invested is 100 percent, or one turn per year. The portion of the total that is circulating capital, amounting to $100,000, will turn over at the rate of 200 percent, or twice a year.

Each of the three elements of circulating capital—cash, receivables, and inventories—will have its own individual turnover rate. Inventory turnover is calculated according to the number of months' supply on hand. A six months' supply would represent two turns per year, or a 200 percent annual turnover rate. Turnover of receivables is expressed as the num-

Figure A-4. **Turnover.**

Basic Relationship

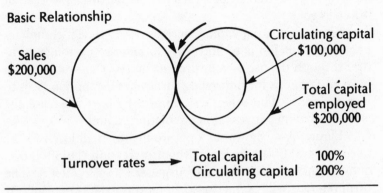

Sales
$200,000

Circulating capital
$100,000

Total capital
employed
$200,000

Turnover rates ⟶ Total capital   100%
Circulating capital   200%

Option A: Increase Sales

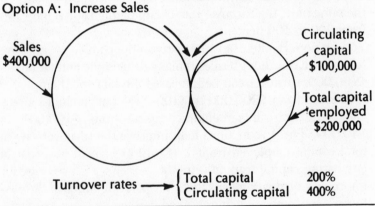

Sales
$400,000

Circulating
capital
$100,000

Total capital
employed
$200,000

Turnover rates ⟶ Total capital   200%
Circulating capital   400%

Option B: Decrease Capital

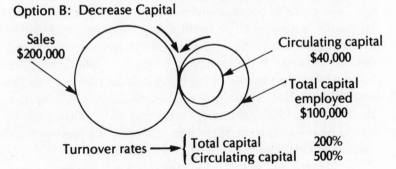

Sales
$200,000

Circulating capital
$40,000

Total capital
employed
$100,000

Turnover rates ⟶ Total capital   200%
Circulating capital   500%

ber of days' business outstanding. If 90 days of business are outstanding, the receivables turnover is four turns per year, or 400 percent.

Since circulating capital increases every time it completes one turn, your job is to find ways to increase customer turnover through the use of your product and service systems. You have two options for improving turnover. One, option A, is to increase sales. The other way, option B, is to decrease the amount of money invested in circulating capital.

Figure A-4 shows an opportunity to double customer sales to $400,000 per year without increasing the $200,000 of total funds employed in the business. This is option A. The turnover rate will be increased from 100 to 200 percent. At the same time, the turnover rate of circulating capital increases from 200 to 400 percent.

Option B offers an alternative opportunity to improve turnover. Even though sales remain at the same annual rate of $200,000, turnover can be increased if total capital employed is reduced from $200,000 to $100,000. This includes a parallel reduction in circulating capital from $100,000 to $40,000. These reductions help improve the turnover rate of total capital employed from 100 to 200 percent and that of circulating capital from 200 to 500 percent. This strategy for improving turnover means that the operating funds of the customer's business are being worked harder.

The profit improvement created by options A and B can be readily appreciated by multiplying the increase in funds generated at each turn of the operating cycle by an increasing number of turns. If the operating profit from one turn in the basic relationship shown in Figure A-4 is $50,000, the profit realized by option A would be doubled to $100,000. In option B, profit would remain at $50,000 but $100,000 of funds would be released from operations that could be used to generate additional business or reduce indebtedness.

Opportunities abound for improving a customer's turnover. The reason is simple. The sum total of funds employed in a customer's business represents the many individual funds that make up circulating and fixed capital. An improvement in the turnover of any one of these funds will correspondingly improve the turnover of the total funds employed. Therefore, you can zero in on any component of a customer's "turnover mix" without having to consider any of the others or their sum total. For example, improvement in the turnover of any single item in a customer's inventory—including your own product—will improve total turnover and consequently contribute to profit improvement.

Contribution Margin

The key to profits is contribution margin—how much margin each product line or business unit contributes to a customer's total profits. Affecting a customer's contribution margins is a key objective. There are two ways to do this. You can help increase sales volume at the current contribution margin. Or you can help increase contribution margin at the current volume of sales.

Figure A-5 shows how contribution margin works. It is calculated by subtracting variable costs from sales revenues. In the example, a customer's total contribution margin is $.095. That means that each single dollar of sales is currently contributing a margin of 9.5 cents to cover the customer's fixed operating overhead of $221,000. It takes a lot of $1 sales to contribute enough 9.5 cents' worth of margins to cover $221,000 of overhead. Even when sales do that, the customer merely breaks even. That is where you come in. If you can increase sales or decrease the variable costs that subtract from sales revenues, you can improve customer profits.

The choices are shown in Figure A-5. If you want to work on product line A, you can improve profits best by improving sales. While it has only a 17.3 percent gross profit, it also has a 9.0 percent contribution. Any increase in sales volume will produce new profits. On the other hand, if you work on product line B, you will have to reduce its variable costs. Its 20 percent gross profit exceeds that of A. But it is making only an 8.1 percent contribution after variable expenses. If you can reduce its expenses, you can improve its contribution even without increasing sales volume.

Measuring Profit Improvement

Customers define a problem as a cost that *can be* reduced or a sales opportunity that *can be* realized. Customers define a solution as a cost that *has been* reduced or sales revenue that *has been* gained. In either case, customer profit has been improved.

Customers measure their solutions according to *incre-*

Figure A-5. Analysis of profit contribution by product line ($000).

	Total	Product Lines		
		A	B	C
1. Sales	$2,600	1,742	650	208
	% 100.0	67.0	25.0	8.0
2. Cost of sales	$2,106	1,440	520	146
	% 81.0	82.7	80.0	70.0
3. Gross profit (1−2)	$ 494	302	130	62
	% 19.0	17.3	20.0	30.0
4. Wages	$ 221	134	65	22
	% 8.5	7.7	10.0	10.5
5. Other	$ 26	10	13	3
	% 1.0	0.6	1.9	1.5
6. Total (4+5)	$ 247	144	78	25
	% 9.5	8.3	11.9	12.0
7. Contribution margin (3−6)	$ 247	158	52	37
	% 9.5	9.0	8.1	18.0

mental analysis. This is sometimes called microanalysis, since it evaluates the new profit earned by a system.

Three methods of incremental analysis are commonly used to measure a system's profit contribution: payback, discounted cash flow (DCF), and accounting rate of return (AROR).

Payback

The payback method measures profit improvement according to how long it will take to recoup the cash outlay required to obtain a system. Payback is essentially a criterion of "cash at risk." If payback can be achieved quickly, the risk factor will be low and the return will be high. If a system's benefits continue after payback, the return will be even higher.

Discounted Cash Flow

The DCF method measures profit improvement by converting the cash values of a system's costs and benefits into a present-time value. Discounted cash flow analysis is usually used in conjunction with payback analysis and the AROR approach on major systems. There are two variations of the DCF method:

1. *Net present value (NPV)* applies a predetermined interest rate to discount future cash flow in order to match it with a system's required cash outlay. The interest rate may be based on a customer's cost of capital or an arbitrary "hurdle rate" that has been set as the minimum payback for new investments. A high net present value is a customer signal to proceed.

2. *Internal rate of return (IRR)* is similar to net present value but does not contain a predetermined discount factor. The IRR is the interest rate that discounts a system's net cash flow to zero present value when compared with its required cash outlay. If the IRR rate exceeds the hurdle rate, a customer will usually proceed.

Accounting Rate of Return

The AROR method measures profit improvement by comparing the average income or expenses saved over the life of a system with the investment outlay required to obtain it. The percentage rate of return that results is based solely on the incremental income generated by the system. It reflects the earnings rate of return on the incremental investment. Many customers favor this method because it is oriented to their balance sheets and income statements even though it ignores the time value of money.

All three measurement methods have certain elements in common. They all use a basic cost-benefit analysis. All of them seek to determine the present value of a system investment on a cash basis, including the opportunity costs involved; the operating revenue; the operating costs; and the difference between operating revenue and operating costs, which equals the benefits.

The ROI Connection

Of the three methods, only the accounting rate of return relates to the return on investment, ROI, which is used to evaluate total customer company performance. This total return on investment must be narrowed down to AROR in order to evaluate an *incremental investment,* such as a specific system. A system's AROR can, therefore, be considered as the added rate of profit that the system can add to the customer's ROI.

AROR/ROI Interrelationships

The interrelationship between ROI and AROR can be seen by the similarity between their formulas:

$$\text{ROI} = \frac{\text{net profit}}{\text{sales}} \times \frac{\text{sales}}{\text{investment}}$$

$$AROR = \frac{\text{net profit}}{\text{investment}}$$

For calculating the accounting rate of return, sales are eliminated from the ROI formula. This is because total customer company analysis is not relevant for most systems investments. The impact of most systems, even huge capital-intensive systems, becomes swallowed up in a customer's total ROI. The consultant cannot identify an individual system's contribution when it is dispersed over such a broad base. Therefore, to make a system's incremental contribution measurable, its impact should be calculated according to AROR.

Net income is not the sole basis for determining AROR. Gross profit may be an appropriate measure of a system's income if no incremental operating costs are involved or if operating costs cannot be separated on incremental sales. Contribution margin may also be an appropriate measure of system income if no incremental fixed costs are incurred or if fixed costs cannot be separated.

System-Opportunity Identification

The return-on-investment approach is the best diagnostic tool to identify opportunities. As the ROI formula shows, opportunity is always present when either a customer's operating profit rate or turnover can be improved.

Any system must meet customer standards of what constitutes an adequate return on investment. A system whose promise of profit improvement falls below this standard will probably be rejected as not being worth the investment. It will usually be ruled out by one of three standards for determining whether a given rate of return on investment is adequate: its investment exceeds the basic cost of money, its payback is too risky, or the return falls below the amount that customers believe they have the right to expect.

The Return-on-Investment Yardstick

To tell whether the increased sales you propose from a profit improvement project are good or poor, you will need an accurate yardstick. In many selling organizations, profit is commonly expressed as a percentage of sales price or as an absolute amount per unit. But any method of measuring profit as a percentage of sales is insufficient for consultative purposes since it takes into account only two elements of profit: sales revenues and cost. The difference between them is then calculated as a percentage of sales. Most companies call that difference profit. Profit, however, has a very important third component: *time.*

From the point of view of return, profit can be regarded as the ratio of income earned *during an operating cycle* to the amount of capital invested to produce it. Thus profits have two costs: time costs and costs of producing the product or service. When profit is compared with its funded investment, it is being expressed as a return on investment, or ROI.

Return on investment is an analytic tool that has three qualities in its favor for your purposes:

1. It is a fair measurement of profit contribution.
2. It is helpful in directing attention to the most immediate profit opportunities, allowing them to be ranked on a priority basis.
3. It is likely to be readily understood and accepted by financial managers as well as sales and marketing managers of your customer companies.

Figure A-6 represents the formulas for calculating return on investment. The formulas relate the major operating and financial factors required in profitmaking to the rate used to measure the profit that is made: the rate of profit per unit sales in dollars, the rate of turnover of operating funds, the funds required to finance business operations, and the total investment of capital employed, including working assets, plants, and facilities.

The customer's sole economic justification for investing in your profit improvement projects is to earn a superior rate of return on the funds invested. This truism must be interpreted in two ways. One is in terms of income gained. The other is in terms of costs avoided in obtaining investment funds, costs of retaining such funds, and costs suffered by denying their use for alternative, potentially more profitable projects.

Figure A-6. **Return-on-investment formulas.**

A. Options for improving ROI by improving turnover

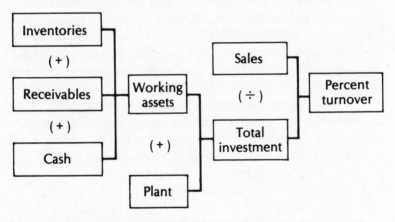

B. Options for improving ROI by improving operating profit

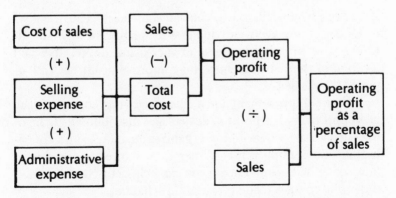

Return-on-Investment Diagnostic Techniques

Diagnosis lies at the heart of consulting. Diagnostic techniques that are based on return on investment lie at the heart of diagnosis.

As Figure A-6 shows, ROI is the product of the rate of operating profit, expressed as a percentage of sales, and the rate of turnover. Any time you want to improve a customer's ROI, you must first diagnose a problem in operating rate or an opportunity in turnover.

Part A of Figure A-6 shows the ingredients of ROI expressed as turnover. If you examine each of those ingredients, you will find profit opportunities that can improve turnover. You can, for example, recommend a project to reduce your customer's receivables. This will reduce the amount of funds invested in working assets, thus reducing the customer's total investment base. As a result, you can improve your customer's profit without increasing sales volume.

Part B shows options for diagnosing profit improvement if your objective is to increase operating profit. You can recommend a project to lower the customer's cost of sales. This will reduce total costs and enable the customer to show an increase in operating profit.

Seeking Simple Opportunities

If you sell to supermarkets, you can show each chain's central headquarters or even individual store managers how substituting your brands for others, or increasing the number and location of their shelf facings, may improve profit per case or per $100 of sales.

Profit improvement for a manufacturing customer may lie in improving the profit of dealers and distributors. By helping a customer's distributor organization increase its contribution—something the customer cannot directly control yet must nonetheless influence—you can help your customer raise the profit on sales made through this channel.

A distributor's largest single investment is likely to be in inventory. The key to distributor inventory control is finding the minimum investment required to maintain adequate sales and service. One way of measuring the utilization of inventory investment is to compare a distributor's inventory turnover with his industry's average. Inventory turnover can be computed by using this formula:

$$\frac{\text{Cost of sales for one year}}{\text{Average inventory}} = \text{inventory turnover}$$

If a customer's distributors are in a business whose inventory turns an average of 4.5 times a year, or once every 80 to 90 days, you can help a distributor whose turnover is lower than average see the problem this way:

$$\frac{\text{Projected cost of sales}}{\substack{\text{Projected average} \\ \text{inventory level}}} = \frac{\$370,000}{\$100,000} = 3.7 \text{ inventory turnover}$$

To help this distributor increase turnover to approach the 4.5 industry average, you will have to help him reduce inventory investment. To do this, you must first find out what level of inventory investment can yield a 4.5 turnover. Divide the distributor's projected cost of sales by the desired 4.5 turnover, which results in an $82,000 inventory. It now becomes clear that you can help the distributor achieve profit improvement by reducing inventory investment by $18,000. Then you can turn your attention to optimizing the inventory mix.

The best approach to inventory reduction is usually through product-line smoothing. Distributors almost always carry too many items in their lines. An inventory burdened by too many items can cause a dissipation of the distributor's sales concentration, extra handling costs, waste through obsolescence or spoilage, and, of course, higher inventory carrying costs, higher insurance costs, and overextended investment.

To analyze a distributor's inventory, you can simply rank the products in the line according to their cost of sales and then compute their inventory turnover. Such an analysis could look like this:

> Products A, B, C, and D account for 57 percent of the cost of sales but only 34 percent of inventory. These products turn over inventory by an average of 6.2 times a year.
>
> Products E, F, G, H, J, and K account for 43 percent of the cost of sales but 66 percent of inventory. These products turn over inventory by an average of only 2.4 times a year.

The inventory turnover analysis in Figure A-7 shows what it costs the distributor to carry inventory. By comparing the carrying costs of inventory to forecast sales volume, you can begin to learn more precisely what inventory the distributor should maintain. The first four products are apparently well controlled. They have an average turnover rate of 6.2 percent and 1 percent average carrying cost as a percentage of

Figure A-7.   **Inventory turnover analysis.**

		Inventory			
Product	% of Sales	Average $	% of Average	Turn-over	Carrying cost as % of sales
A	15	7,000	7	8.2	0.8
B	17	9,000	9	7.0	0.9
C	14	11,000	11	4.7	1.3
D	11	7,000	7	5.8	1.1
Subtotal	57	34,000	34	6.2	1.0
All Other Products	43	66,000	66	2.4	2.6
Total	100	100,000	100	3.7	1.7

sales. You now know that you must concentrate on reducing inventory whose average turnover rate is only 2.4 percent and average carrying cost is 2.6 as a percentage of sales. This will help bring the distributor's inventory down to the $82,000 level that should contribute to the projected 4.5 inventory turnover.

Appendix B

The Assessment Process for Approving Capital Expenditures

The capital budgeting process contains four steps:

1. Project planning
2. Evaluation and decision-making
3. Control and audit of cash commitments
4. Postaudit evaluating and reporting of results

The first step proceeds on the assumption that a company has a formal long-range plan or, at the least, the proposed project fits into the mainstream of the corporation's interest. Implicit in a proposal is a forecast of markets, revenues, costs, expenses, profit. These aspects of capital budgeting are the most important, most time-consuming, most critical phase, and largely outside the expertise of the financial executive. A major project generally affects marketing, engineering, manufacturing, and finance.

The uncertainties surrounding a long-range forecast are often great enough to throw doubt on the effectiveness of the entire decision-making process. Probability analysis of success or failure becomes important in view of the uncertainties. A relatively simple approach to evaluating uncertainty is discussed later. However, sophisticated probability analysis and computer simulation can be beneficial in giving credulity to major long-range projections in the face of great uncertainty. Unless this phase of capital budgeting is made reliable and meaningful, the decision-making phase becomes simply an exercise in arithmetic.

The second stage, project evaluation and decision-making methods, has received major attention in accounting and financial publications. There is general agreement that the time-adjusted cash flow methods (net present value and discounted cash flow [DCF] rate of return) are the most meaningful guides to the investment decision; however, there is still a place for cash payback analysis in appraising the financial risks inherent in a projection. These methods will be examined and brought into perspective for use in the proposed model. Within certain limits, and where they can be identified, these measures will give the best tools for appraising proposals. They do not produce the magic go/no-go answer. They give management guidance. No matter what quantitative guidelines are developed, qualitative factors will be important in the final decision—the personal judgments and preferences of the project sponsor and management cannot be discounted.

The third step, control and audit of cash, is the simplest step in the budgeting process once the source of funds has been determined and committed. After approval, the project should be treated as any other budgeted item, with payment schedules determined and variances reported and explained. Major overspending can impair the validity of the investment decision, and even invalidate the entire process.

A caution is appropriate at this point. When a proposal calls for a specific investment, it is implicit that no more than that amount will be spent. Overspending of any significant amount cannot be permitted. Similarly, a project sponsor should not come back the next year for additional funds because he underestimated his original request. When either of these events occurs, it becomes necessary to refigure the entire project on the total cash outlay. Unfortunately, at this point the firm is already irrevocably committed to the project and the new calculations are after the fact.

Everyone agrees that the fourth step, postaudit evaluating and reporting of results of investment, needs doing, but rarely is it done. As we will see below, capital investments are projected on an incremental basis, on a cash basis, and on an internal rate of return basis over the life of the investment. Regular financial records and reports are on an annual basis, an accrual basis, or on a rate of return by individual years. A major problem is that many projects become an integral part of a larger, existing investment and the new project cannot be separated from the existing one. The postaudit of the incremental segment may become obscure or meaningless. As a result, many incremental investments cannot be appraised against objectives—for example, a large rate of return. The large projected incremental rate of return may become diluted when merged with a larger investment. There may be general disappointment because the new investment results have not lived up to forecasts and yet the projected earnings and cash flow of the incremental investment may be right on target.

New criteria for postaudit may have to be determined to affect postaudit for many projects at the time the original projections are made so that management knows how it will measure results against plan. One criterion may be cash flow. Another criterion may be the development of pro forma statements comparing financial income before and after the additional investment; that is, a financial model. The main point is that good budgeting calls for comparisons of projections and results, and though the project evaluation criteria may not be susceptible to audit in many cases, it should not preclude the establishment of other criteria for postaudit purposes at the time the original projection is made. The use of pro forma statements indicating total results as well as impact on earnings per share before and after the investment may be the appropriate basis for appraisal of the additional investment.

Principles of Capital Investment Analysis

This section describes the specific concepts used to evaluate major capital expenditure projects and programs within the scope of the capital budgeting process. The underlying concepts and methods used are examined to bring into focus the economic consequences of a capital expenditure.

When a capital expenditure is proposed, the project must be evaluated and the economic consequences of the commitment of funds determined before referring it to a budget committee for review or to management for approval. How are the economic consequences described best? This is done in two steps:

First, set up the project into a standard economic model that can be used for all projects no matter how dissimilar they may be.

$$\text{Benefits} - \text{cost} = \text{cash flow}$$

To describe the formula in accounting terminology:

Benefits: Projected cash revenue from sales and other sources

Costs: Nonrecurring cash outlays for assets, plus recurring operating expenses

Cash flow: Net income after taxes plus noncash charges for such items as depreciation

Thus, if the model were stated in a conventional accounting form it would appear as:

Add: Cash revenues projected (Benefits)
Less: Cash investment outlay and cash expenses (Costs)
Total: Cash flow

The "benefits less costs" model is usually developed within the framework of the firm's chart of accounts and supported with prescribed supplementary schedules that show the basis of the projection.

It should be apparent that in setting up an economic model, the conventional accrual accounting concept of net income after taxes has been abandoned. The established criterion is cash flow—net income after tax plus noncash charges.

Second, adjust the cash flow into relevant financial terms. The cash flow projected for each year over the life of the proposal has to be translated into financial terms that are valid; that is, translate the annual dollar cash flows to a common dollar value in a base year. This concept must not be confused with attempts to adjust for changes in the purchasing power of the dollar.

The calculations assume no significant erosion in the purchasing power of the dollar. Should this occur, the time-adjusted common-dollar concept may require adjustments for the diminished real value (purchasing power) of future dollar payments. The common dollar value concept used in capital budgeting adjusts for time value only. This is achieved through the development of the concept of discounting and present value that will be examined in the next section. An examination of how a simple two-step model is developed will illustrate the rationale of this approach.

In the first step we set up the economic model: benefits minus costs equal cash flow. To complete this model we need to identify in detail all economic benefits and costs associated with the project. Benefits typically take the form of sales revenues and other income. Costs include nonrecurring outlays for fixed assets, investments in working capital, and recurring outlays for payrolls, materials, expenses, and so on.

For each element of benefits and costs that the project involves, we forecast the amount of change for each year. How far ahead do we forecast? For as long as the expenditure decision will continue to have effects; that is, for as long as they generate costs and significant benefits. Forecasts are made for each year of the project's life; we call the year of decision "Year

Zero," the next year "Year One," and so on. When the decision's effects extend so far into the future that estimates are very conjectural, the model stops forecasting at a "planning horizon" (ten to fifteen years), far enough in the future to establish clearly whether the basis for the decision is correct.

We apply a single economic concept in forecasting costs: opportunity cost. The opportunity cost of a resource (asset) is what the company loses from not using it in an alternative use or exchanging it for another asset. For example, if cash has earning power of 15 percent after taxes we speak of the cash as having an opportunity cost of 15 percent. Whenever an asset is acquired for a cash payment, the opportunity cost is, of course, the cash given up to acquire it. It is harder to establish the opportunity cost of committing assets already owned or controlled. If owned land committed to a project would otherwise be sold, the opportunity cost is the after-tax proceeds from the sale. The opportunity cost of using productive equipment, transportation vehicles, or plant facilities is the incremental profit lost because these resources are unavailable for other purposes. If the alternative to using owned facilities is idleness, the opportunity cost is zero. Although opportunity costs are difficult to identify and measure, they must be considered if we are to describe the economic consequences of a decision as accurately as possible. An understanding of this concept of opportunity cost is probably the most critical to this economic analysis.

At the end of the first step we have an economic model for the project's life, showing forecast cash flows for each year. In the second step we convert the results into financial terms that are meaningful for decision-making. We must take into account the one measurable financial effect of an investment decision left out in Step 1: time. Dollars shown in different years of the model cannot be compared since time makes them of dissimilar value. We clearly recognize that if we have an opportunity to invest funds and earn 15 percent a year and if we have a choice of receiving $1,000 today or a year from now, we will take the $1,000 today, so that it can be invested and earn $150. On this basis, $1,000 available a year from now is worth less than $1,000 today. It is this adjustment for time—discounting—that is required to make cash flows in different years comparable.

This time value of funds available for investment is known as the opportunity cost of capital. This should not be confused with the cost of raising capital—debt or equity—or with the company's average earnings rate. Like the opportunity cost of any resource, the opportunity cost of capital is what it will cost the company to use capital for an investment project in terms of what this capital could earn elsewhere.

The opportunity cost of capital is alternatively referred to as the minimum acceptable rate of interest, the marginal rate of interest, the minimum rate of return, the marginal rate of return, and the cost of capital. Whatever the term used, and they are used loosely and interchangeably, it reflects the rate the corporation decides it can be reasonably sure of getting by using the money in another way. It is developed through the joint efforts of management, who identify relevant opportunities, and the controller, who translates management's judgment into a marginal rate.

Another simple economic concept must be introduced: incremental cost, sometimes called differential cost or marginal cost. By definition it is the change in cost (or revenue) that results from a decision to expand or contract an operation. It is the difference in total cost. In performing the capital budgeting analysis we deal with incremental costs (revenues) only. Sunk or existing costs are not relevant to the evaluation and decision.

Throughout this discussion, all references to costs and revenues are on an incremental basis.

Rationale of Discounting and Present Value

Discounting is a technique used to find the value today (the "present value") of money paid or received in the future. This value is found from the following formula:

Future dollar amount × discount factor = present value

The discount factor depends on the opportunity cost of capital expressed as an interest rate and a time period. Table B-1 illustrates how discount factors are usually displayed. The discount factors are grouped according to the annual interest rate, expressed as the present value of $1.00, and then listed according to the year the amount comes due. The table should be read this way: when a dollar earns 10 percent per year uniformly over time, a dollar received at the end of the second year is equivalent to (worth) about 86 cents today.

Arithmetic and Concept of Present Value

To adjust the model's results for the time element we "discount" both the positive and negative cash flow forecasts for each period at the company's marginal rate of return to determine their present value. This discounting process makes the forecasts equivalent in time. We can now add the present values of these cash flow forecasts to derive the net present value (NPV). The NPV is a meaningful measure of the economic consequences of an investment decision since it measures all benefits and all costs, including the opportunity cost of capital.

Table B-1. Present value of $1.00 at 10 percent.

Year	Present Value (Today's Value)
0–1	$0.9516
1–2	0.8611
2–3	0.7791
3–4	0.7050
4–5	0.6379

When the net present value of a proposed investment is determined we are ready to decide whether it should be accepted. This is done by comparing it to the economic consequences of doing nothing or of accepting an alternative. The general rule followed in comparing alternative projects is to choose the course of action that results in the highest net present value.

Table B-2 illustrates the cash flow forecasts and time-value calculations for a typical proposal to invest in a new project when the alternative is to do nothing; that is, maintain liquidity rather than invest. A discount rate of 10 percent is assumed as the company's marginal rate.

The proposed project will cost $500 in year 0, and cash operating expenses thereafter will be $200 per year for four years. Assume the cash benefits will be positive but decline over the four years and total $1,450. The cash flow is negative in the year of investment but positive in the succeeding years and there is a net positive cash flow over the life of the project of $150 before discounting. When the cash flow forecasts are made equivalent in time by multiplying each annual cash flow by the present value of the dollar for each period, the time-adjusted cash flow is determined, and the net present value is found to be $60. The proposed investment is better than

Table B-2. Arithmetic of determining net present value.

Year	Benefits	Costs	Cash Flow	PV of $1 @ 10%	Discounted Cash Flow
0	$ 0	$ (500)	$(500)	1.000	$(500)
0–1	425	(200)	225	.952	214
1–2	425	(200)	225	.861	194
2–3	350	(200)	150	.779	117
3–4	250	(200)	50	.705	35
Total	$1,450	$(1,300)	$ 150		$ 60 NPV

doing nothing since all costs are covered, the 10 percent opportunity cost of the corporation's funds is realized, and in addition, the project will yield an additional $60 return.

Table B-2 indicates an NPV of $60. Depending on the cash flow or the discount rate, the NPV could be negative or zero. If the NPV were zero, the company would have projected earnings exactly equal to its marginal rate of 10 percent. If there were no alternative projects, and the only alternative were to do nothing, the project with the NPV of zero would be accepted since the company would earn its marginal rate of return. (As explained later, the NPV of zero would yield the discounted cash flow rate of return; that is, 10 percent.) If the NPV were negative because of an inadequate cash flow, assuming the same 10 percent marginal rate required by management, it would mean the project would earn less than 10 percent, and it would be rejected.

A number of evaluation methods are employed in capital budgeting; however, after critical examination of all methods, only the arithmetic developed in this simple model will be used to examine three methods used in evaluating capital budget proposals: (1) cash payback, (2) net present value, (3) discounted cash flow (DCF) rate of return, sometimes referred to as the "internal rate of return."

Cash payback is commonly used by businessmen evaluating investment opportunities, but it does not measure rate of return. It measures only the length of time it takes to recover the cash outlay for the investment. It indicates cash at risk. In our model there are costs of $500 committed in year 0. To determine payback we merely add the unadjusted cash flow for each year and determine how many years it takes to get the outlay back. In the first two years $450 is recovered, and by the end of the third year $600 is recovered. By interpolation we find cash recovery to be approximately 2.3 years. It is obvious that the rational businessman does not commit large sums of money just to recover it. He expects a rate of return commensurate with the risks and his alternative use of his funds in alternative investments (opportunity cost). In our example the calculation of payback reveals a relatively short exposure of funds and cash flow continuing beyond the pay-back period. It is interesting information in overall project evaluation, but not conclusive. Our model will automatically throw off payback as a byproduct as we calculate the crucial time-adjusted net present value of the investment and DCF rate of return.

A version of cash payback that has come on the scene recently to aid in the evaluation of ultra-high-risk investments is described as the cash bailout method. This approach takes into account not only the annual cash flow as shown in Table B-2, but also the estimated liquidation value of the assets at the end of each year. If the liquidation value of a highly spe-cialized project is zero, then cash payback and cash bailout are the same. But if it is assumed in our example that the liqui-dation value of the investment at the end of year 1 will be $275, the cash bailout would be one year (cash flow $225 plus liquidation value $275 = $500 original cash commitment).

We consider net present value as described a valid basis for determining the economic consequence of an investment decision. Many business economists use it as their sole crite-rion for the go/no-go decision for investment. We recognize this method as paramount throughout our analysis but prefer using it in conjunction with other measures rather than as the sole criterion.

Arithmetic and Concept of Discounted Cash Flow Rate of Return

We are now ready to examine the concept of DCF-ROR. It is completely different from the return on investment (ROI) commonly used by businessmen. The conventional ROI is computed for an accounting period, generally on the accrual book figure; investment is taken at original cost (sometimes at half original cost); no adjustment is made for time value when looked at in the long run.

We are talking about a very different rate of return on investment—the discounted cash flow rate of return in the interest rate that discounts a project's net cash flow to zero present value. Let us expand Table B-2, which shows a $60 NPV when a discount factor of 10 percent is used, to Table B-3, which adds a discount factor of 18 percent and yields a $0 NPV.

The DCF rate of return is 18 percent. By definition the DCF-ROR is the rate of return on the project determined by finding the interest rate at which the sum of the stream of after-tax cash flows, discounted to present worth, equals the cost of the project. Or, stated another way, the rate of return is the maximum constant rate of interest the project could pay on the investment and break even. How was the 18 percent determined? By trial and error.

Many analysts use the net present value method exclusively; some use the DCF rate of return; others use the two methods to complement each other. Using NPV, positive or negative dollar values are determined with the cost of capital as the benchmark. Excess dollar PV is evaluated and a judgment is made. The DCF rate of return approach ignores the cost of capital in calculation and determines the rate of return on the total cash flow. The result of this approach on our example is to convert the $60 NPV into a percentage. It works out to 8 percent on top of the 10 percent that had been calculated for the NPV. Many businessmen prefer working with

Table B-3.   Arithmetic of determining DCF rate of return.

Year	Cash Flow	PV of $1 @ 10%	Discounted Cash Flow	PV of $1 @ 18%	Discounted Cash Flow
0	$(500)	1.000	$(500)	1.000	$(500)
0–1	225	.952	214	.915	206
1–2	225	.861	194	.764	172
2–3	150	.779	117	.639	96
3–4	50	.705	35	.533	26
Total	$ 150		$ 60 NPV		$ 0 NPV

the single figure of 18 percent for evaluating a project against a known cost of capital, instead of describing a project as having an NPV of $60 over the cost of capital. It is our feeling that the two methods complement each other, and under certain circumstances one may give a better picture than the other.

Let us reexamine this special DCF rate of return to see what distinguishes it from the conventional rate of return. It is time-adjusted to base year 0, so that all dollars are on a common denominator basis; it is calculated absolutely on a cash flow basis; the investment is a definite time-adjusted value; the rate of return is determined at a single average rate over the total life of the investment. Certain implications of this statement require explanation.

The DCF rate of return is calculated over the full life of the project and the accountant's yearly ROI cannot be used to test the success or failure of the new investment. If the planned life of a project is ten years, and if it can be segregated from other facets of the operation, the DCF rate of return has meaning only when the full economic life of the project is completed. However, in this case it is possible to monitor results on a year-to-year basis by examining the actual dollar cash flow and comparing it with the projected cash flow. (Observe the assumption that the project is separate and distinct from the rest of the operation.)

The one thing that disturbs businessmen most about the DCF rate of return concept is the underlying mathematical assumption that all cash flows are reinvested immediately and constantly at the same rate as that which yields a net present value of 0. In our example in Table B-3, 18 percent was used as the discount factor as a constant. Another case could just as easily have indicated at 35 percent rate of return, with the implicit assumption that the cash flow was reinvested at 35 percent. But if the earning experience indicates a cost of capital of 10 percent, how can we reconcile the assumption that we can continue to earn 35 percent on the incremental flow?

Even though a firm's average earnings reflect a cost of capital of 10 percent, the demands on incremental new investment may well have to be 18 to 35 percent to compensate for investments that fail to realize projected earnings. As long as opportunities are available to invest at an indicated 18 percent or 35 percent, it does not follow automatically that it is inconsistent with the average earnings of 10 percent. However, if it is felt that a projected rate of return of 18 percent, in our example, is a once-in-a-lifetime windfall and no new opportunities can be found to exceed the average 10 percent rate, then we are in trouble with our DCF rate of return concept. The reinvestment rate will not stand up. In this situation we have to combine both net present value and rate of return to explain the situation in this way: the 10 percent rate of return of this project covers the opportunity cost of money and throws off an additional $60 cash flow. If other projects of the same magnitude can be found so that the total cash flow generated can be reinvested at the same rate, there would actually be a rate of return on the project of 18 percent (the DCF rate of return). The lack of other good investment opportunities is a constraint on the full earning capacity of the project.

We have examined three methods of evaluating investment opportunities. Cash payback evaluates money at risk. Present value measures the ability to cover the opportunity cost of an investment on a time-adjusted basis of money and indicates by a net present value whether the project under consideration will yield a "profit" or a "loss." The discounted cash flow rate of return is an extension of the net present value concept and translates it into a single rate of return that when compared with the opportunity cost of capital gives a valid basis for evaluation.

Since NPV and DCF-ROR concepts take into account the opportunity cost of capital through the discounting technique, it may be stated as a principle that all projects under consideration where this opportunity cost is covered should be accepted. This proposition is both theoretically and practically sound, but three factors need to be considered: How do you determine the minimum acceptable rate of return (the opportunity cost of capital) to select the proper discounting factor? How can you assume no constraints on the supply of capital so that all worthwhile projects can be accepted? How do you take risk into account when examining indicated results? These questions will be examined in the next three sections.

Minimum Acceptable Rate of Return—Cost of Capital

How do you determine the minimum acceptable rate of return (cost of capital) used in discounting? Again a caution: the cost of capital concept used here is not the same as the cost of borrowing. This is probably the most critical factor in the evaluation process. It is a unique and personal rate to each company. There is no guide to look to in other firms. Two firms looking at a potential investment, say an acquisition, may place two completely different values on it. To Company A, with a minimum required rate of return of 10 percent, the investment could be attractive, while to Company B, with a required rate of return of 25 percent, the investment would be totally unacceptable. The difference is centered in the cost of capital to each firm, its opportunity rate of return—the rate that can be expected on alternative investments having similar risk characteristics. An example of the arithmetic involved in reaching this conclusion can be seen when we modify Table B-2 to include both a 10 percent and 25 percent discount factor and assume that both companies A and B are the potential sole bidders for an investment with an asked price of $500 and a net cash flow of $150. (See Table B-4.)

The investment is very attractive to Company A but completely unacceptable to Company B—it would realize less than its objective of 25 percent. If Company A were in a position to know the cost of capital of Company B, it would know that Company B would not bid at all for this investment. Company A would know that it would be the sole bidder.

If a company has successfully earned 25 percent on the capital employed in the firm, an investment opportunity to be attractive would have to yield at least that rate. The 25 percent

Table B-4. **Comparison of NPV using 10% and 25% discount factors.**

Year	Cash Flow	(A) PV of $1 @ 10%	Discounted Cash Flow	(B) PV of $1 @ 25%	Discounted Cash Flow
0	$(500)	1.000	$(500)	1.000	$(500)
1	225	.952	214	.885	199
2	225	.861	194	.689	155
3	150	.779	117	.537	81
4	50	.705	35	.418	21
Total	$ 150		$ 60 NPV		$ (44) NPV

represents the cost of capital to that firm and an investment opportunity offering only 15 percent would be rejected. A second firm with a 10 percent cost of capital would find the same 15 percent potential attractive and accept it. Thus the same 15 percent opportunity investment is attractive to one and unattractive to the other. Both firms analyzing the identical situation reach different logical conclusions.

Cost of capital in our analysis is *always* considered to be the combined cost of equity capital and permanent debt. We evaluate economic success or failure of a project without regard to how it is financed. Yet we know that money available for investment is basically derived from two sources: debt with its built-in tax saving so that its cost can be as little as half the market price for money (depending on the tax rate), and equity, which has as its cost the opportunity cost of capital of the owners.

It is necessary at times to break down the combined cost of capital into its components (cost of debt capital and cost of equity capital) to put it in terms understandable to the businessman who commonly measures results in terms of return on equity. To illustrate this cost of capital concept, we will assume that a corporation is owned by a single individual

whose investment objectives are clearly defined. The total cap-
italization of the firm is $100, made up of $30 permanent debt
capital and $70 owner's equity capital. If preferred stock was
outstanding at a fixed cost, it would be treated the same as
debt. The after-tax interest rate of the debt money is 2.75
percent. The after-tax dollar return on the combined debt and
equity capital of $100 under various operations would appear
as shown in Table B-5.

Restating these dollars as rates of return on the investment of $100, $30 debt and $70 equity, the percentage return
on capital would be shown in Table B-6.

Table B-5.   After-tax dollar income on investment of $100.

Income on Total Investment (Before Interest)	$30 Debt × 2.75% Cost of Debt Capital	$70 Equity Income on Owner's Equity
$ 8.00	$0.825	$ 7.175
9.00	0.825	8.175
10.00	0.825	9.175
11.00	0.825	10.175
12.00	0.825	11.175

Table B-6.   After-tax rate of return on investment of $100.

Rate of Return	Cost of Debt Capital	Rate of Return on Owner's Equity
8%	2.75% ($0.825 ÷ $30)	10.25% ($7.175 ÷ $70)
9%	2.75%	11.68%
10%	2.75%	13.11%
11%	2.75%	14.54%
12%	2.75%	15.96%

If the company has been earning an average of $10 on the total investment of $100, and the cost of debt is $.825, the earnings on owner's equity is $9.175. Stated as a rate of return, the $10 earned on $100 is 10 percent return on the total investment (combined cost of capital), and because of the leverage built into the capital structure with long-term debt, the $9.175 earnings on equity yields a return on equity of 13.11 percent (cost of equity capital). When there is a 30 percent debt structure and the average cost of debt is 2.75 percent after taxes, we can readily convert return on total investment into return on equity by reading our table. It is quite simple to create similar tables for each company and its debt/equity ratio (for example, with a 50/50 ratio and debt cost of 2.75 percent, a 10 percent return on total investment yields a 17.45 percent on equity capital). If there is the opportunity to invest the company funds in alternative situations, or reinvest the funds in the business and continue to earn at least 10 percent on the combined debt and equity funds, we would describe this as the opportunity cost of capital. This is the critical rate used in discounting: the discount rate used to determine net present value and the benchmark for comparing discounted cash flow rate of return are based solely on the combined cost of capital. The rate of return to the stockholder can be derived and compared with his opportunity cost; that is, his ability to invest his funds elsewhere and earn at least the same rate.

Having decided that return on combined capital is the appropriate criterion for evaluating investment, it is necessary to follow through with this concept when projecting revenues, expenses, and net benefits. If we are to determine net benefits (cash flow) on combined capital, all charges against that capital must be excluded from the expense projections. If interest were charged in the projection, there would be double charging. This is not a novel method; it is used regularly by investment analysts who often determine income before interest on funded debt and before taxes.

As noted, interest expense on long-term debt is not included in the current expense projection because it is covered in the combined cost of capital computation. The interest on short-term debt may be a direct charge to operations if its cost is not in the invested capital base. If the major financing is handled through equity and long-term debt and the short-term borrowing is negligible, this method is acceptable. However, many companies live off their current borrowings and the short-term debt is actually part of the permanent capital. The true leverage would then be reflected in the return on owner's equity when compared with the return on total investment. Again a caution: when this method is used, the interest expense on current debt must be excluded from projected costs.

The capital funds of a company constitute a pool of monies for all projects. A particular borrowing rate for additional capital, at a time when a new project is introduced, becomes part of the pool of funds and it becomes part of the average cost of debt relative to total capital. With the addition of new funds it is the average long-run cost that is significant and not the current borrowing rate. The relevant comparison of the projected rate of return is with the average rate for the pool of funds and not the cost of the incremental funds.

In the case of the individual ownership of a corporation, the historical earnings rate can be determined along these lines and a cost of capital for opportunity cost evaluation can become a valid benchmark. If average earnings rise from $10 to $12 there is a new cost of capital, a new cutoff rate for accepting or rejecting projects. This does not imply constantly changing cutoff rates. Some years will be more profitable than other years, some years the cost of debt may be higher or lower than other years, but the earnings of the company are the average adjusted for trend. There is not much logic in setting a cutoff rate at 25 percent when the average is 10 percent just because there was once an isolated year that had unusually high earnings. Many good projects would be rejected because of an unrealistically high cutoff point. The reference point should be actual accomplishment and reasonable expectations, not wishful thinking.,

When the assumption of the individual ownership of a corporation is abandoned in favor of a public corporation with a myriad of stockholders, the cost of capital concept gets into difficulty. It is difficult enough postulating the opportunity cost of capital for even a small family, but when we try to postulate the investment objectives of all the different stockholders in a large corporation things become really complex. One stockholder wants cash dividends; another wants growth and reinvestment of earnings; still another wants fast capital appreciation. The opportunity cost of capital to each owner becomes indistinguishable. We are not going to grapple with the problem of cost of capital for publicly owned corporations here because it is a problem that is extremely complex and can be highly theoretical. It is sufficient to note that some large public corporations have been able to develop a cost of capital for their capital budgeting evaluations with some success. Other public corporations have conceded that they cannot develop a cost of capital for all their stockholders and have resorted to a cutoff rate commensurate with their earnings experience. This latter approach violates the opportunity cost concept for the individual owners, but practical considerations have made it necessary to recognize the opportunity cost of the corporation as a person with only minor reference to the real persons who own the firm.

Constraints on Supply of Capital

How can you assume no constraints on supply of capital for investment? Theoretically, if the earnings of a corporation are great enough, and growing fast enough, there is no limit on the amount of debt and equity available. In good basic economic theory, firms should continue their capital expansion until the marginal cost of capital equals its marginal revenue; or stated simply, it is worth borrowing as long as the earnings exceed the cost by even a small amount. The principal limit on debt to the successful corporation becomes the ability of the management to live with it—at what point do the managers start losing sleep because they are so heavily leveraged? However, there are other practical constraints. General business conditions and the state of optimism or pessimism may lead to a limit on the amount of capital a management is willing to commit. There are constraints on the amount of risk a management may be willing to assume; there may be limits on the ability of an organization to handle certain ventures. There are probably other constraints, real and imaginary. In the budgeting process all categories of investments must be classified and weighed. The degree of risk that is tolerable, and a commensurate return, exist only in the mind of individual managements.

There is no nice formula that can set this. Depending on the management's philosophy, and assuming constraints on availability of capital, the selection may result in the rejection of good safe investments promising a 10 percent return, and acceptance of promotional investments with a great risk promising a 60 percent return, and vice versa. Another constraint mentioned is organization, which may be the decisive factor in choosing between an investment that will make few demands on management and one that will make great demands on management. The latter may offer a superior projected return, yet it may be rejected, reluctantly, because management does not have confidence in its ability to cope with it even though the indicated economic rewards are greater. The practical problems of project selections are varied and complex. While the techniques discussed are hardly the *sine qua non,* they do lend objectivity and direction.

Describing Risk and Uncertainty

How do you account for risk in evaluating the net present value or DCF rate of return? A more accurate term is uncertainty, but risk and uncertainty tend to be used interchangeably by businessmen. The technical difference between the two terms is found in the ability to determine probability of future outcome. Risk, with respect to outcome, implies that future events can be determined within a range of known probabilities, while uncertainty implies that probabilities of outcome cannot be established. Not all proposals have exactly the same element of risk. One investment risk category, the outlay of funds to introduce labor-saving equipment, can be evaluated quite accurately; the projected benefits may be almost a certainty.

Management could even decide to accept all such proposals where indicated NPV exceeds the combined cost of capital. Another category of risk may be the introduction of new product lines. The difference in uncertainty between the two categories is obvious. There probably would be no blanket acceptance of proposals for new products at the cost of capital cutoff rate.

The discount factor remains constant no matter what the risk. The recognition of the different risk categories results in a subjective evaluation of the uncertainties of the venture and a markup on the cost of capital for the go/no-go decision. For example, with a cost of capital of 10 percent, a proposal is made to invest in replacement equipment. There is a modest NPV, little uncertainty. All such proposals would be segregated and acted upon and probably accepted. The second situation, introducing a completely new line or lines whose success is highly uncertain and producing a modest positive NPV, would hardly be acceptable. All such risky proposals would be segregated and judged individually within this special group. To compensate for the uncertainty, a minimum acceptable cutoff rate may be two or three times the cost of capital rate. Average success or failure may actually fall to the 10 percent average cost of capital to the firm.

The determination of the projected rate of return on an investment from the NPV can be arrived at by raising the discount rate until the NPV is zero. This is the DCF rate of return, which is the projected average return on the investment. If such a rate came to 18 percent against a cost of capital of 10 percent, it is still left to the judgment of management whether the additional 8 percent rate of return is adequate to cover the uncertainty of success or failure. This is how risk is usually evaluated—purely subjectively.

There are more exact and sophisticated methods that we will describe. Risk implies probabilities of success or failure.

The fact that the project evaluation method we describe here is quite precise and yields a definite answer must not blind us to the reality that decisions are always made in the face of uncertainty. The rate of return description of a project's economic consequences is a single, uncertain prediction of projected revenues and expenses. We cannot ever completely remove this uncertainty. The best we can do is to describe the probable range and intensity of uncertainty involved and the economic consequences of forecasting errors. Next, we briefly discuss two methods that have been found helpful in performing this work.

Sensitivity Analysis

Sensitivity analysis seeks to determine how much a project's net present value or DCF rate of return will be affected (its "sensitivity") when a single factor, or specific group of factors, changes by a given amount. Let's say that for a given project we have been able to predict the volume of product sales with relative certainty, but the price forecast remains very doubtful. To make a sensitivity analysis we would repeat the evaluation using different prices; this would show how much the NPV changes with each price change.

When used with discretion, the results of sensitivity analyses are helpful in estimating the economic consequences of specific forecasting errors. As a minimum requirement, each project evaluation should describe the effect of a wrong forecast in the factor or factors judged most uncertain. However, with analysis of this type we are measuring the effect of change of a single factor or groups of factors while all other factors in the projection are held constant. When other components of the projection change, and they are ignored, the new answers may have serious limitations. For example, to change projected prices but to hold volume and costs constant may be unrealistic. We become "practical" at this point and settle for simple sensitivity analysis and get rough answers because manually reworking the model to reflect all possible changes in the figures to determine new cash flows becomes an almost impossible task. In this area computer programs really become significant. Hundreds of single factors can be tested against all other factors and the arithmetic can be worked accurately in minutes instead of in weeks.

Probability Adjustment

Probability is the preferred method of organizing estimates of both the range and intensity of uncertainty for the decision-maker. In using this method the decision-maker computes a reasonable range of possible outcomes for the economic model from very unfavorable to very favorable. He then estimates in his own mind the probability that each will occur. If the unfavorable outcome seems more probable than the favorable one the project is probably unwise, and vice versa.

An example of probability analysis after the initial projection has been made can be prepared as a test of its validity. No one can forecast with complete confidence and certainty the annual cash flows resulting from projected volume, prices, or even costs. The probability of achievement can be examined by preparing a table of possible deviations from the forecast. Assuming the initial annual cash flows had been projected at $10,000, a reappraisal by management might indicate the following possible results:

5 chances in 100 annual cash flow will be $14,000
25 chances in 100 annual cash flow will be   12,000
45 chances in 100 annual cash flow will be   10,000
20 chances in 100 annual cash flow will be   8,000
5 chances in 100 annual cash flow will be   0

It is apparent that the projected $10,000 annual cash flow has been reassessed as being the most probable, and that there is also an indication that there is a 30 percent chance that it will be exceeded. However, there is a 20 percent chance that it will be less, and a 5 percent chance it will fail completely.

There is no precise formula for testing the validity of the judgments that lead to predictions of chances of success or failure. They are based upon subjective judgments of experienced and responsible executives. If this type of analysis does nothing more than force an orderly reappraisal of a project, it will serve its purpose. In this example, the conclusion may be that the $10,000 annual cash flow forecast looks reasonable and the initial projection would be allowed to stand. If on the other hand the probabilities of achieving less than the $10,000 had been greater, it would probably lead to a writedown of the cash flows.

The introduction of probability analysis also opens the way to very sophisticated statistical analysis of projected results. Computer programs have been developed that measure probabilities of success or failure of the principal factors making up the projection (volume, prices, costs, etc.), and it is possible to determine projected results taking into account any combination of favorable and unfavorable events. The DCF rate of return is then stated as rates over a range of probabilities. This approach may be extremely beneficial in evaluating major projects, but one must bear in mind that the mathematics is still based on human judgments of chances of success or failure.

Project Evaluation

Evaluating components of an investment program for a firm is complex at any time. There are many categories of investments: (A) revenue-producing projects, (B) supporting facilities projects, (C) supporting services projects, (D) cost-savings projects, and (E) last but hardly least, in this era of air and water pollution control, investment required by public authority that will yield no return. Each must be evaluated to determine its incremental consequence.

When a project is isolated from the rest of the operation, evaluation is relatively clear. But sometimes a planned major investment embraces several auxiliary projects which, evaluated by themselves, are not very meaningful. When this occurs, it is necessary to construct a master model that includes all of the projects. Some of the auxiliary projects may not come into being for several years after the main investment is made, and may or may not produce a net positive cash flow. The master model in simple form may take on the appearance shown in Table B-7 if individual projects of the types *A, B,* and *C* are assumed (the figures do not add up; only format is demonstrated).

If the three projects are interrelated, they should be projected as a single entity. In our example, *A* is assumed to be a major facility that to be successful needs *B* added in three years as supporting facilities; *B* would have no basis for existence if *A* were not created. Project *C* may possibly be identified as a new computer information system that will produce only costs, but would not exist if *A* and *B* were not created. All costs and all benefits for all corollary investments need to be projected as far into the future as possible to get a true evaluation. Investment evaluations that are made of a project with all the certainty of a DCF percentage can be grossly misleading if the supporting investment of satellites is not taken into account. Actually, these are not separate investments. There is only one: Project *ABC.* The evaluation has to be of the new single entity. The postaudit can be of only the conglomerate single entity, *ABC.*

Projects of the cost-savings category, *D*, are generally easiest to identify and evaluate. There are relatively clear-cut choices: invest $40,000 today for new labor-saving machines that will reduce labor costs $12,000 per year; the machines

Table B-7.   Master project.

Project	NPV	0	1	2	3	4	5	---	15
A	100	(30)	(2)	14	14	13	13		40
B	40	—	—	(15)	5	5	5		20
C	(26)	—	(2)	(2)	(4)	(4)	(4)		(10)
Total	114	(30)	(4)	(3)	15	14	14		(50)

will last eight years, and quality of performance will be unchanged. Determine the NPV and/or DCF rate of return and accept or reject. Such investment opportunities constantly arise, but it is almost impossible to project them as part of a master project. As a result, such investments are evaluated as isolated investment opportunities that may occur in three years, or eight years, or never. When they occur, if of major proportions, they affect the potential return on the total investment.

A cost-incurring project, *E,* such as spending $100,000 to prevent air pollution or being closed up, is one of the few black-and-white decisions a businessman faces. He decides to go on. Ideally he would expense it. He may have to capitalize it and write it off, and in addition have annual related operating expenses. This nondiscretionary investment falls into the same general category as type *C,* support project. The cash flow is always negative and must be included as an integral part of the master investment. If the commitment is large enough, it may sharply reduce the original projection and a revision may be necessary.

Selecting Among Projects

On the basis of the techniques for evaluating planned capital investment, it is now possible to move to the methods of selecting among projects. As noted above, in theory, selecting among projects is easy. Invest in anything that when discounted at the appropriate marginal rate will yield a positive NPV. Practically, for many reasons, there are constraints on capital in the minds of most managers. Let us look at the project selection problems that are involved for projects under consideration in a particular risk category when there is a limit on capital.

We have selected the NPV method as the best approach to analyze proposed projects of varying lives. Comparing projects under the DCF-ROR method can be misleading because of the different life factor and the reinvestment factor inherent in each ROR. Excess NPV avoids this difficulty. When the various projects are converted into a profitability index, selection is further facilitated. The profitability index is the ratio of the NPV to investment. For example:

$$\frac{\text{Present value of expected benefits}}{\text{Investment}} = \frac{\$132,000}{\$100,000} = 1.32$$

In selecting projects when a limit is imposed upon the amount available for investment, we look for the combination that will maximize combined net present value without exceeding the imposed limit. We know that we have reached this goal when we can no longer increase the combined net present value by substituting one project for another and still satisfy the constraint.

A way to achieve a satisfactory combination of projects is through trial and error. As a guide we can use the profitability index (see Table B-8). However, such ratios are not foolproof. This is illustrated where there are three possible projects requiring a total of $1,500 in initial outlays, but where $1,000 is the imposed limit.

The choice is investment in $A + C$ (cash outlay $1,000) and $B + C$ (cash outlay $900). Since $A + C$ have a combined greater NPV than $B + C$ ($1,500 versus $1,200), $A + C$ should be selected even though C's ratio (1.25) is less than B's ratio (1.40). Such differences are common. The profitability

Table B-8.   Profitability index.

Project	Net Present Value		Investment: Cash Outlay		Profitability Index
A	$1,000	÷	$600	=	1.67
B	700	÷	500	=	1.40
C	500	÷	400	=	1.25

index must always be used judiciously. When there are numerous projects to choose among, the combining process becomes more difficult.

Summary

After examining working concepts of what is involved in the capital budgeting process, you can appreciate the many problems that must be resolved when attempting to be "objective" and "scientific" in capital commitments. The first step is planning the new investment. This is critical. Investments with long life expectancy are wrapped in a shroud of uncertainty, yet plans and projections based on intuition and a minimum of facts are often made with an aplomb that gives the impression of certainty. Hard conclusions and decisions are often reached on the basis of very soft facts. The recognition of uncertainty and its proper evaluation are probably the most important steps in the analysis of an investment. Yet this is the area where we often become "practical" because the task is so difficult, both in the gathering of the necessary data and its evaluation. If all the sophisticated measures of evaluating uncertainty are attempted manually, the paperwork literally becomes overwhelming and it becomes advisable to turn to computer programs for help with the mathematics.

The use of the computer is becoming accepted practice in the capital budgeting procedure. The description of the manual methods of computation already presented, and those that follow in the model, assume an aura of certainty. Every attempt is made to approximate the greatest probability of certainty, yet the calculations that evolve from a single measure must be evaluated in the light of uncertainty. The computer programs based upon sensitivity analysis, decision tree analysis, and probability analysis that have been mentioned can now extend our computational abilities.

A program based on a technique known as "Monte Carlo Simulation" makes possible the "simulation" of future events by sampling values from our estimates under favorable and unfavorable circumstances and making all necessary cash flow calculations by random chance. This is an important step forward in the sophisticated handling of uncertainty based upon the principles we have very briefly examined. Suffice it to state at this juncture that where computational speed and accuracy are beneficial, computer programs based upon sound theory and principles exist or are being developed. Our primer has recited the principles on which programs have been developed and can be employed advantageously in many situations.

After the development of a plan on an incremental basis, we spent a good deal of time developing and examining recommended criteria for evaluating projected investments. A simple two-step model was developed. The first step, with three elements, is applicable in all situations:

Benefits less costs equals cash flow

This is the basis for preparing all projections. The next step is to adjust the cash flow to eliminate time differences. All cash flows are adjusted to year zero, which becomes the common denominator for evaluations. The adjustment is made by discounting future values to present values. The mechanics of discounting are not difficult to master but the determination of a discount factor is. The discount factor is the interest rate that equates with the firm's combined cost of capital. This is a relatively new concept and should not be confused with the traditional cost of borrowing. Cost of capital is the rate earned on the combined capital of equity holders plus the permanent debt used as part of the capital of the firm. This simple explanation stands up for the firm with a sole owner who can evaluate the rate of return with his own opportunity cost of capital. When a public corporation becomes involved, the calculation of equity cost of capital could become extremely complex if an attempt were made to take into account the opportunity costs of the various stockholders. For our examination we have simplified the problem by recognizing a combined cost of capital where opportunity costs can be determined. This rate becomes the discount value and is used for discounting.

When proposed investment benefits are discounted at a rate consistent with cost of capital, we have a net present value that tells us that the project will yield more or less than the cost of capital. This rate becomes our cutoff rate when considering whether to accept or reject. Many analysts use this NPV as the sole criterion for evaluation of the project. We recognize the importance of NPV but carry it a step further to discounted cash flow rate of return (DCF-ROR) because the latter changes the excess NPV dollars to a single percentage rate of return that is often easier to comprehend. These two measuring devices that are time-adjusted through the discounting methodology are teamed up with several other criteria to bring the maximum information to bear on the analysis. The most prominent of these is cash payback, which is introduced to reflect money at risk only, and not a rate of return. All these calculations were built on judgments by responsible executives. The final calculations are presented to a budget committee for its appraisal of the facts. The validity of the mathematics used in the projecting and final evaluation is dependent on the skill, objectivity, and integrity of the men making the multitude of subjective judgments that are needed at many stages in the development of the projection.

When an NPV or DCF-ROR is determined for a project and the company's alternative to investment is to do nothing, the choice is clear. When the choice of capital commitment is among several projects and there is a limit on the amount of capital available for investment, we have chosen to compare projects using NPV rather than the DCF-ROR. We are not committed to saying NPV is better than DCF-ROR in all situations, or vice versa. Each has features that work better in some situations.

We recognize the need to control authorized cash expenditures once a commitment is made. Projections of NPV or rate of return are made. If cash expenditures exceed estimates, the projected benefits are meaningless. Practically, this has been a pitfall for many good capital budgeting procedures. If large overexpenditures are made, a new projection should be prepared; however, this yields a new rate of return only after the fact. By that time we are merely generating statistics.

Postaudit of investment is difficult. It is often neglected. If a plan of postaudit is not determined and agreed upon at the time a commitment is to be made, the probabilities are there won't be one or one will be attempted and may not be satisfactory. As all investments are projected on an incremental basis, and the results are usually part of a larger investment, there is an inability to sort out the results of the incremental portion and identify its NPV or DCF-ROR. It is not fair to management, and it is poor budgeting procedure, to establish a value upon which important decisions are made and then announce you cannot compare the results with the budget. NPV and DCF-ROR indicate expected results over the complete life of the investment, but there is a desire and need to appraise results on an annual basis. For those investments that can be identified apart from other investments, the postaudit can be in the form of tests of cash flow and adjusted financial statements. When the investment becomes an integral part of existing investments, the incremental portion cannot be identified and plans must be made to postaudit on the basis of the new combined investment. This will involve the preparation of a master investment projection at the time the incremental investment is planned. A financial model should be prepared, combined cash flows can be computed if desired, postaudit can be performed for the master investment. It is important that this step be taken, or the failure of postaudit is almost a certainty.

Index